"THE *SALESMAN* HAS A BIRTHDAY"

Essays Celebrating the Fiftieth Anniversary of
Arthur Miller's
Death of a Salesman

Edited by

Stephen A. Marino

‖‖‖‖‖‖‖‖‖‖‖‖‖‖‖
D1715963

University Press of America, ® Inc.
Lanham • New York • Oxford

Library of Congress Cataloging-in-Publication Data

"The Salesman has a birthday" : essays celebrating the fiftieth anniversary
of Arthur Miller's Death of a salesman / edited by Stephen A. Marino.
            p. cm.
Papers originally presented at the Fifth International Arthur Miller Conference
in April 1999 at Saint Francis College in Brooklyn Heights, N. Y.
            Includes bibliographical references and index.
    I.   Miller, Arthur, 1915-Death of a salesman—Congresses. I. Marino,
Stephen A. II. International Arthur Miller Conference (5th : 1999 St.
            Francis College (Brooklyn, New York, N.Y.)
    PS3525.I5156D4373 2000 812'.52—dc21   00-021212 CIP

            ISBN 0-7618-1653-4 (cloth: alk. ppr.)
            ISBN 0-7618-1654-2 (pbk: alk. ppr.)

                PS
                35 25
                ,I 5 156
                D4373
                2000

⊖™ The paper used in this publication meets the minimum
requirements of American National Standard for Information
Sciences—Permanence of Paper for Printed Library Materials,
ANSI Z39.48—1984

To my wife, Katie,
and my children,
Addie, Molly and David,
for their love and understanding

Contents

Preface

To mark the first anniversary of the Broadway opening of the original production of *Death of a Salesman*, Arthur Miller wrote an essay entitled, "The *Salesman* Has a Birthday," which appeared in the *New York Times*, February 5, 1950. Miller reflected: "So what is there to feel on this anniversary? Hope, for I know now that people want to listen. A little fear that they want to listen so badly (12)." Fifty years later, Miller's reflections are just as relevant.

Since its Broadway opening on February 10, 1949, *Death of a Salesman* has been recognized as a landmark of twentieth century American drama. Clive Barnes recently has called the play "one of the major texts of our time, a watershed in drama, not just of historic value, but of sustained, if varying, pertinence" (Post 38). Its status as a world play was confirmed when *Salesman* was ranked second to Samuel Beckett's *Waiting for Godot* in a millennial project survey of theater professionals conducted by England's Royal National Theatre to celebrate the best 100 plays of the twentieth century. In the same survey, *The Crucible* was ranked sixth and Miller was named the top English language dramatist.

The significance of the fiftieth anniversary of the original production of *Death of a Salesman* has been celebrated by scholars and critics, and highlighted by a new production of the play which opened at the Eugene O'Neill Theatre on February 10, 1999, exactly fifty years after the original debut. This critically-acclaimed production, which came to Broadway by way of the Goodman

Theatre in Chicago, received three Tony Awards: Best Revival of a play, Best Lead Actor for Brian Dennehy's performance as Willy Loman, and Best Featured Actress for Elizabeth Franz's re-defining role as Linda Loman. At the award ceremony, Arthur Miller accepted The Lifetime Achievement Award. The New York production amassed box office records for a straight play as a new audience of theatergoers, students, and critics experienced *Salesman.* Miller's reflection on the first anniversary still stands fifty years later: "People want to listen."

The essays in this collection are gathered from papers delivered at the Fifth International Arthur Miller Conference in April 1999 at Saint Francis College in Brooklyn Heights, New York—the same neighborhood where Arthur Miller lived as a young playwright, husband and father in the 1940s and 1950s. The conference's theme, "The *Salesman* Has a Birthday," focused on the significance of the play's fiftieth anniversary, its importance in the American dramatic literary canon, and its relationship to Miller's oeuvre. Christopher Bigsby's keynote address, "Arthur Miller: Time Traveller," traces Miller's interest in time as a continuum in his more than 60 year career. Matthew Roudane analyzes how the play constructs borders, boundaries, and thresholds. Brenda Murphy offers a critical commentary of the 1999 production. Peter Levine examines *Salesman* as a part of American culture. Steven Centola shows how Miller structured the play as a unity of oppositional forces. Heather Cook Callow argues how traditional boundaries between masculine and feminine are broken in the play. George Castellitto asserts that the tension between Marxism and Capitalism in American society forces Willy Loman to the crisis which results in his suicide. My essay probes the importance of Brooklyn as the setting of *Salesman.* Susan Abbotson discusses Lyman Felt in *The Ride Down Mt. Morgan* as the dramatic heir to Willy Loman. Jane Dominik examines the thematic and structural similarities between *Salesman* and other plays in Miller's canon.

During this anniversary year, Miller spent much time in newspaper, magazine, and broadcast interviews reflecting on the significance of *Salesman's* milestone. He also produced a number of his own essays, most notably a new preface for the 50th anniversary edition of the play in which he admits he "cannot find a means of absorbing the idea of half a century rolling away beneath my feet" (ix). In addition, Miller sent a thoughtful message about *Salesman* to the conferees gathered in Brooklyn. His remarks, which began the proceedings, reveal how he has been absorbing the impact of the original and current productions of the play:

> I find it curious that the Society should be meeting around the corner from my old home on Willow Street where I lived for many years until the mid-Fifties. I did a lot of wandering about in the neighborhood a long time ago, and now there you are talking about the work I was never sure I'd get done. We are forever unknowingly walking over the threads of others' memories, entangling our own with theirs. The transiency is all...in America, anyway.
>
> Your being on Remsen Street naturally reminds me of my time on Brooklyn Heights, and the years spent assaulting the theatre. Without an off-Broadway theatre to speak of you had to find Broadway production, a very doubtful triumph for my kind of plays. My attitude toward Broadway was a mixture of the contemptuous and the envious. In truth, though I may have been jealous of some of its skillful practitioners, contemporary theatre never satisfied. It was too true to life and too uninterested in the spirit; I recall thinking that all the important things were between the lines, in the silences, the gestures, the stuff above or below the level of speech. For a while I even thought I ought to study music, which is the art of silences hedged about by sound. Music begins *Salesman*, and not by accident; we are to hear Willy before we see him and before he speaks. He was there in the hollow of the flute, the wind, the air announcing his arrival and his doom.
>
> Just this morning a student called from Ann Arbor with some questions for an article she was doing, and asked if I had so to speak designed Willy to be "universal," as she put it, or for that matter some of the other people in my other plays. But how can one plan such a thing? I wasn't even sure the play would see production! What it never occurred to me to doubt, however, was that there was one humanity, albeit with very different etiquettes and styles of life and speech. And so the play was not addressing some better-educated or sophisticated sector of the audience but more people more or less like my own father who expected a performance to kidnap his imagination and carry him away. Without in any way suggesting comparisons, the great Greek and Elizabethan plays were written for demotic audiences and were intended to be embraced by every level of society, and so it may be that universal works spring in

some part, from their creators' relations with a broad audience to begin with. Of course nothing guarantees anything.

The public's reception of this new *Salesman* is rather phenomenal; they tell me it is the most successful straight play in memory, with a run projected into next Winter. The narrowing of audience's attention-span seems not to have affected this audience. Maybe it only referred to the attention span of the critics. I can't pretend, in any case, to understand what there is about the Lomans that has kept them from fading away, but I confess to speculating about this occasionally.

It does make me wonder whether we are all forever being hunted, pursued by one or another sloganeered meaning, one or another packaged view of life and death which in our weakness we surrender to when in the privacy of our midnights what we most long to find is the freedom to be and believe everything. Maybe that is what Willy does, since he is all mood, all feeling, a naked branch of an old tree swaying in the wind. Willy moves with the air and from one moment to the next, one feeling to the next, and in a sense believes everything at once...that he is loved, that he is contemptible; that he is lost, that he has conquered; that he is afraid, that nothing frightens him and that everything does, and on and on and on. It may be that he has escaped the categories simply because he is a human, and too self-absorbed to be embarrassed at being one. Whatever else you may say about him, he is unmistakably himself...even including the times when he wishes he wasn't.

I am up here, two hours plus from Brooklyn, trying to keep my vow not to abandon my desk for a while. The trip eats up a day, there has been one interruption after another in the past months, going back to last Fall's production of *The Ride Down Mt. Morgan* at the Public with Patrick Stewart...who incidentally will open it on Broadway this coming February.

So I must ask you to accept my apologies for my absence; I am pleased and more than flattered at your interest in my work. I write this after breakfast, trying to fight off a morning nap, and recalling some of the old Greeks writing plays into their late eighties and nineties, and hoping that they also tended to doze off with pen in hand. In short, I need the day and wish you all the best of life.

Arthur Miller
April 13, 1999

At this writing, the new production of *Death of a Salesman* has just closed its nine-month New York run and will move to London where Miller's reputation is arguably greater than in his native country. Afterwards, the play again will be consigned to future audiences who will surely discover its original power. As Fintan O'Toole observed: "This play was great in 1949 and will still be great in 2049" (53). Certainly, future audiences will be moved simply because they will be human beings who will still want "to listen badly." They, too, will be awed by the terrible thing happening to the Loman family. As Ben Brantley observed during the opening night of the new production: "I could hear people around me not just sniffling but sobbing. I feel sure that audiences for *Salesman* will be doing the same thing 50 years from now" (E1).

Stephen Marino
Saint Francis College
November 1999

Acknowledgments

I would like to thank Arthur Miller for his permission to reprint his opening remarks. I would also like to express my gratitude to Dr. Frank Macchiarola, President of Saint Francis College, for his permission to hold the Fifth International Arthur Miller Conference at the Brooklyn campus. I must also recognize Ann Amore, Vice-President for College Relations, and Petra Ludwig, Director of Special Events, for their vital help and support in organizing the conference. Special thanks to Eric Hafker for his editing. I would also like to acknowledge the advice and encouragement of Steven Centola, the founding President of the Arthur Miller Society.

Arthur Miller: Time Traveller

Christopher Bigsby

In an article published in *Harper's* Magazine, in March 1999, Arthur Miller insists that:

> There is no such thing as 'reality,' in any theatrical exhibition that can properly be called a play. The reason for this is that stage time is not, and cannot be, street time. In street time, Willy Loman's story would take sixty-two years to play out instead of two and a half hours...with the very act of condensation the artificial enters even as the first of its lines is being written (38).

Time and reality, then, are intimately related, while to enter a theatre is to acknowledge that we enter a time warp in which the normal laws of physics no longer apply. Time flows at a speed determined by the author. The price of entry into this world is that we experience a temporal anomaly in which past and present may co-exist within a factitious moment. And few writers have been as interested in time, and its various ramifications, as Arthur Miller—time, that is, as history, time as memory, time as a component of identity, as productive of guilt, nostalgia, hope, psychological and social imperatives. Even his concern with shaping language, with moulding speech into distinctive rhythms, is an aspect of his concern with time for, as Sam Shepard has remarked, "rhythm is the delineation of time in space" (Lippman 11).

In his preface to *Salesman at Fifty*, Arthur Miller says, "As far as I know, nobody has figured out time. Not chronological time, of course—that's merely what the calendar tells—but real time, the kind that baffles the human mind" (ix). The remark is made in the context of his amazement at the passage of fifty years since writing his classic play but it goes a good deal deeper than that in so far as time is a recurring concern, device, paradox, metaphysic in his work, the mechanism of causality, the source of reproach, irony, metaphor. In a country where eyes are resolutely fixed on tomorrow, on the green light across the bay, the orgiastic future, he insists on the authority of a past which can be denied only at the price of true identity and the moral self. And in some sense Miller has worked against the American grain.

The American writer, he insisted, behaves as though "the tongue had been cut from the past, leaving him alone to begin from the beginning, from the Creation and from the first naming of things seen for the first time...It is as though they were fatherless men abandoned by a past that they in turn reject" (*Timebends* 114-5). It was Ralph Waldo Emerson who insisted that, "Time and space are but physiological colors which the eye makes," and who asked, "Whence ... this worship of the past." It was he who insisted that "...history is an impertinence and an injury, if it be anything more than a cheerful apologue or parable of my being and becoming" (Morse 28-9). And the central American project, as Willy Loman well knew, was precisely about the connection between being and becoming, the necessity to deny the past in the name of his and his culture's manifest destiny to colonise the future, a process which it is assumed will gift the individual and the country a true identity. As Jonathan Morse observes, in his book on the language of memory, *Word by Word*, when President Bush was asked before his 1989 inaugural to comment on his campaign rhetoric of the previous year he replied, "That's history. That doesn't mean a thing anymore" (69). It was a very American statement, fully in line with Hester Prynne's pronouncement that, "Let us now look back...The past is gone! Wherefore should we linger upon it now" (Hawthorne 173). History, in other words, leaves no residue. It is used up. It exists only to be invalidated by time. The myth of American society is that the journey to America was a double journey, forward to the future but also back through time towards innocence, a world free of history and ultimately, of course, of time, a movement which logically washed the individual free of responsibility and hence a utopianism stained at source. That was the double journey identified at the end of *The Great Gatsby*. It was a journey into myth and myth exists outside of time. To Arthur Miller, on the contrary, history makes authentic demands, and history provides a spine to mere events. As he has said, "Chaos was life lived oblivious of history" (Martin 80). But this was not history as a fast-receding present. His sense of history was akin to that of T.S. Eliot who spoke of "the historical sense ... a perception, not only of the pastness of the past, but of its presence" (32). Interestingly, Eliot made that remark in the context of his essay on "Tradition and the Individual Talent." In that essay he insisted that:

> The historical sense compels a man to write not merely with his own generation in his bones, but with a feeling that the whole of the literature of Europe from Homer and within it the whole of the literature of his country has a simultaneous existence and composes a simultaneous order. This historical sense, which is a sense of the timeless as well as the temporal together, is what makes a writer traditional. And it is at the same time what makes a writer most acutely conscious of his place in time, of his own contemporaneity (38).

It is in that sense, and perhaps that sense alone, that Miller, who sees the Greek theatre as at one with his own, who has spoken of his acute sense of the contemporary but also his sense of the timeless as well as the temporal, of simultaneity, is traditional. He is traditional, in other words, in Eliot's sense of a writer with an awareness of the presence of history. For Eliot, the past must live "not merely [in] the present, but the present moment of the past...conscious, not of what is dead, but of what is already living" (44). Explaining further what he means Eliot observed that "the difference between the present and the past is that the conscious present is an awareness of the past in a way and to an extent which the past's awareness of itself cannot show (39). It is a remark that is simultaneously banal and, in the context of a lecture on Miller and time, a useful reminder of the sense in which history operates in Miller's work. It is not only that the present interrogates the past for a meaning which only becomes apparent with the passage of time but that the present already contains the past whose shape and form it tries to measure.

Miller has never written a play set in the past if it has not served the presence of that past. He is not, in other words, an historical dramatist in the sense that Gore Vidal is an historical novelist. With William Faulkner's Gavin Stevens, he insists that "the past is never dead. It's not even past" (Faulkner 81). It is a truth that Willy Loman knows all too well, while desperately denying. L.P. Hartley's *The Go-Between* famously begins, "The past is a foreign country. They do things differently there." For Arthur Miller, the past is far from a foreign country. They do things in much the same way and that is its utility. In Miller's work the significant fact is not the difference between past and present but the continuity, the causal, moral connection, the concurrence of what *was* with what *is*.

John Fowles called his recent collection of essays, *Wormholes*. At a time when more people speak Klingon than Esperanto, there is no need to explain that, especially to Trekkies like yourselves. It refers to the "hypothetical interconnection between widely separated regions of spacetime" (Fowles xii). So that it is possible, virtually instantaneously, to move from one space-time to another. It is essentially what Miller implies in the title of his autobiography *Timebends*. It is the mechanism behind *Death of a Salesman, After the Fall, Clara, The Ride Down Mt. Morgan, Mr. Peters' Connections* and *Timebends* itself, all of which fold time together, bring past and present into immediate contact. And the assumption behind that is that meaning is a product of such interactions, that the parallel universes of 'now' and 'then' once brought into contact, generate significance, speak to one another in the language of memory.

Wormholes are not theoretical interconnections. They exist. We can already move instantly to another space-time. The mechanism for that journey is, in one sense, the theatre itself, and, in another sense, memory. Different times and places are brought together in an instant and theatre, with its power to transform space and time, becomes itself a paradigm. In *Salesman* the two—theatre and memory—come together as the play recapitulates not only the processes of memory but the processes of art as Willy Loman constructs a past, trying to find form in contingency, a logic in mere event, a character and an identity in incidents and social relationships, a connection, in short, with his own life. In effect he is the author of much of *Death of a Salesman* as Tom is the author of Tennessee Williams's *The Glass Menagerie*, in that he constructs the text out of the memories he chooses to recall and in part remake. To a degree he writes the script and performs himself quite as if it were indeed a play and he an actor, albeit one who has lost the attention of his audience. He is like John Osborne's Archie Rice in *The Entertainer*: he has lived on beyond the moment when his particular skills can command attention—and for an actor attention, attention must be paid. In the same way Miller constructs Willy Loman as a fictional marker in his own desire to make sense of a culture, to render up a coherent personal and public meaning.

Willy does bear the marks of the past. He reaches back, in memory and language to the days of the frontier, and Miller has said that, "It was part of his nature, to me, that he sprang from people who were wandering in the mountains" (Bigsby *Interview*). But he also, in his occasional linguistic formality, aspires to what Miller calls "a more elegant past, a time 'finer' than theirs," that offers a dignity he feels he lacks. Thus Miller draws attention to Willy's remark that he had "been remiss," not a Brooklyn locution, and not, incidentally, a Jewish locution. He is, indeed, in Miller's telling phrase, "light years away from [the] religion or community [that] might have fostered Jewish identity" (*Salesman at Fifty* xii). He is, in other words, stranded in time and space and stripped of an identity that could only have come from acknowledging the authority of the past and the necessities of the present rather than the seductive light of a golden future. He is, Miller suggests, instead, "on the sidewalk side of the glass looking through at a well-lighted place" (*Salesman at Fifty* xii). He is mesmerised, separated from the reality of his own being, as he stares at a life he can envisage but not reach, a world that exists, tantalisingly, on the other side of a transparent membrane, a future he can see but cannot reach. And perhaps it is worth recalling that the phrase "a well-lighted place" has echoes of Hemingway's short story about a suicidal old man kept alive by a comforting and consoling vision.

But when does this play, written both by Miller and, in part, at least at the level of narrative assumption, by Willy Loman, take place? What is its time? What Miller has said of *Elegy for a Lady* he could have said of *Salesman* and, incidentally of *Mr. Peters*, but also, in a sense, of many of his plays. It takes place, he has said, "in the space between the mind and what it imagines" (Martin 427). Indeed, asked when *Salesman* was set he replied, "All I can tell you is that I think it is suspended outside of chronological time" (*Salesman Notebook*). And, of course, you will remember that one of its titles was to have been *A Period of Grace*, a reference to that anomalous period in which the time of an insurance policy has expired but it continues, temporally, with no temporal referent. Just how much this play is "suspended outside of chronological time," however, can be told from the notebook he kept while writing the play. In this he writes of Willy, "He is fired, or the Depression hits." The Depression? But isn't this supposed to be 1948 or 1949? Yet there is something of the Depression about Willy's fear of losing his job, though, in fact, at the age of sixty-three, he is only two years from retirement and the mortgage is about to be paid. The play, Miller confesses, "is a bit like a dream. In a dream you are in two places at the same time and *Salesman* is in two places at the same time" (*Interview*). The wormhole. He could almost be talking about *Mr. Peters' Connections,* which is equally suspended in time, "a bit like a dream" and which, as its title implies, concerns a man's attempts to trace the connections which could be said to give some kind of coherence to his life, connections that he seeks through memory, different moments in time brought together in a moment outside of time.

But, then, time, to Miller, is an agent of connectiveness, a clue to the hidden code of experience, that connectiveness which generates social, individual and moral coherence. As he wrote in a note to himself:

> Life is formless—its interconnections are concealed by lapses of time, by events occurring in separated places, by the hiatus of memory. Art suggests and makes the interconnections palpable. Form is the tension of those interconnections, man with man, man with the past and present environment. The drama at its best is a mass experience of this tension (*Notebook*).

Those connections across time are the essence of coherences in individual lives but they are also a primary motive and method in Miller's work. He bends time in the belief, for example, that history does, indeed, have lessons to offer. When Cortes confronts Montezuma in *The Golden Years*, the space-time continuum is

breached in a number of ways. Indeed when the play opens, the
threat is of an end to time as the sun goes into eclipse, an eclipse
which Montezuma and his followers believe may mark the
apocalypse and which does, in fact, foreshadow the eclipse of an
entire culture which is about to suffer as time runs out on their
civilisation. Beyond that, not merely do two different times, two
different histories, two different modes of being come together in a
moment which is both in time and outside of time, which is to say
within a myth, but an arc of electricity shorts across time and space,
through the wormhole linking 16th century Mexico to 20th century
Europe. In that sense, though in a different way, we are once again
"in two places at the same time." Miller wrote of Montezuma's
paralysis in the face of the implacable power of Cortes because, at the
end of the 1930s, he saw the same thing as the western powers
appeared transfixed by the sheer fact of Adolf Hitler. As he has said,
he always requires a present need as a justification for writing of past
events. The same kinetic energy surges through the wormhole from
1692 to 1953 in *The Crucible* while the mere title of *The American
Clock* should alert us to the significance of time in a play in which, as
he has told us, he went "in search of those feelings that once ruled
our lives and were stolen from us by time."

   The American Clock was in part inspired by Studs Terkel's *Hard
Times*, described by Terkel as "a memory book" (93). In a note he
insisted that it was "a book about Time as well as *a* time" (iv). It was
a book about Time in the sense that it was a collection of testimonies
by what he called "an improvised battalion of survivors," testimonies
in which the passage of time had transformed fact into memory. As
he warned, "in their remembrances are their truths" (3) and memory
has a problematic relationship to truth. Memory is, after all, not a
time capsule, suddenly revealing a fragment of the true past. The
story of *a* time is thus subject to the alchemical force of passing time,
memory being selective, bearing the impress of a transformed self.
Time, in other words, is intensely subjective. As Miller has said,
"Memory inevitably romanticizes, pressing reality to recede like
pain" (*Timebends* 179). That is true of Studs Terkel's respondents,
as it is of Willy Loman who Miller has identified as a romantic.

   But again, *The American Clock*, written in the late 70s, opened a
wormhole onto another time, the 1930s, beginning, though, with a
glimpse at the 20s when time appeared to have no meaning. As a
character observes, "They believed in the most important thing of

all—that nothing is real! That if it was Monday and you wanted it to be Friday, and if enough people could be made to believe it was Friday—then by God it was Friday" (*Clock* 10). They believed that "for them the clock would never strike midnight, the dance and the music could never stop." In 1929 the clock struck, and reality returned and it was to remind people of that reality, of the fact that we live in time that he wrote the play at the end of the 1970s because:

> It seemed to me that we had completely lost any historical sense. We continually seem to devour or wipe out the past. Consequently there is always a grasping for some kind of handhold on reality...I think we just do not give a damn about what happened. It is mildly interesting. Occasionally you see an old car and think, oh, that's the way they used to make cars...But any old idea, any old way of life is of no conceivable use... So I thought it would be interesting to paint a canvas of life thirty or forty years ago.

Why? Because, as he said, "This [the 1930s] is when there was such a thing as necessity," and in the 1970s this truth of the 1930s seemed to have been forgotten. The two things, therefore, had to be brought together. The 1930s had to appear through the swirling spiral of the wormhole.

And that same wormhole effect, that same bringing together of different times, was true across a whole range of his plays. *A Memory of Two Mondays,* for example, is set in what Miller calls "bygone days," clearly, from internal references, the 1930s when he, like his characters, worked in an auto parts warehouse, but it is a play for the 1950s. As he explained:

> What it is saying to the mid-1950s, which the mid-1950s chose not to hear, was that this was the bedrock. While we were busy doing this boom there were a lot of people in warehouses who were condemned, as though to death, by an economic system from which there was no recourse for them, and that they were what you might call important people. They were not supposed to exist, so it was news from the nether world...Of course, nobody could be less interested in such events in the mid-fifties when the tail-fins were going on to cars, television was roaring up, Eisenhower was in heaven, and all was well with the world.

Thus memory, his memory, becomes an agency of moral and social value as the 1930s and the 1950s are momentarily linked, the 1930s boldly go through the wormhole to encounter the 1950s. The same logic, he has suggested, applied to *Incident at Vichy*, set in Vichy France, but about "today" and to *Broken Glass* set in 1938 but written at a time of revivified fascism in Europe and the "ethnic cleansing" of the former Yugoslavia. And the link between widely separated regions of space time is evident in other ways in that play as Sylvia feels a sudden, inexplicable and paralysing link with events in another place, Europe, while from another time come memories which offer a further explanation for her physical paralysis. But of course memory, as Studs Terkel warned, is not an objective truth. It is deformed, reshaped, decontextualised, prized free of its temporal location. Past events, actions, emotions are recalibrated, re-tuned. They are dissected in search of some meaning that is less imminent than revealed by the polarised light of passing time and present need. And that is true of *Salesman*, a play which, as he has said, is "full of the concrete evidences of living in this country but...is also suspended over all that. It transcends all that."

Memory is important in a number of ways to Miller. I once started to research Miller's family in Poland, only to realise that the Nazis not only killed the Jews, they systematically destroyed the archives which registered their individual and collective histories. They wished, in other words, to annihilate memory and identity as, in seeking later to destroy the evidence of their crimes, they sought to deny responsibility for their actions. They conspired against history. They killed time. No wonder, then, that memory, identity, moral responsibility, denial, betrayal, became central themes of Miller's work or that time, folding back on itself, becomes a distinguishing tactic of his drama. Memory is not a device for Miller. It is a moral responsibility. As he has said, "I think the job of an artist is to remind people of what they have chosen to forget."

In *Playing for Time*, adapted from Fania Fenelon's book about her experiences in Auschwitz, the protagonist exists in a world in which time is effectively suspended as she is lifted out of normality and relocated in a world in which causality itself seems inoperative. Here she plays for time, in the sense that she plays to stay alive, she buys time by playing in the camp orchestra. The time signature of the music constitutes the alternative rhythm by which she lives. She becomes a Sheherazade, with music rather than words being the mechanism of survival. Sheherazade tells stories in order not to be murdered and story is a device for resisting death, for denying mortality, as, of course, it is for all writers who seek to win some final victory over time by the act of writing, by the construction of an alternative universe immune, like Keats's Grecian urn, to the depredations of time if not to the ironies generated by the contrast between art and the human agency that creates it. Yet, for Fenelon, as for Miller, the memory of that time is crucial and hence both in turn lay that time before this one, bring it through the wormhole so that, in the theatre, we see that other time, so that these ghosts from the past breathe our air as, for a moment, we breathe theirs and hence acknowledge, at least within the factitious present of the theatre, our co-presence and hence immediate affinity. Time and space collapse into a singularity. That singularity is the play.

Time haunts Willy Loman. The memory of what was collides with a knowledge of what is. He is supremely conscious of what G.J. Whitrow, first President of the delightfully named International Society for the Study of Time, called the thermodynamic arrow of time, characterised by a tendency towards disorder. For Willy, yesterday's open country has become today's oppressive urban reality. Yesterday's dreams have deferred to today's disillusionment. Then the family would climb into the car to ride to Ebbets Field and glory; now he prepares to ride to his death alone. Yesterday's bright hopes can now be carried in two battered suitcases. They contain his life. Then, the world was charged with energy and he at its heart, the hero of his own story. Now, entropy rules. Once-new machines are in a state of collapse. A golden boy has become a disillusioned man as Willy, once the principal in his own life and the centre of attention, now finds himself pressed to the margin, leaching energy.

Unable to change his present he re-imagines the past which becomes simultaneously pregnant with possibility and the prelude to despair. In the past the season is always spring, with elm trees in leaf and lilacs in bloom. But this was the time when lilacs last in the dooryard bloomed. Something has died, in Willy Loman and the society he believes himself to serve. In the present grass will no longer grow. Seeds fall on barren ground. The elm trees have been cut down to make room for apartment houses. Bewildered by such spiralling decline, by the eclipse of youthful dreams, struck by the irony which is underscored by the now permeable membrane between past and present, he retreats not so much into a real past as a past

past charged with nostalgia. He is a romantic, like F. Scott Fitzgerald's Gatsby, and just as unaware of the collateral damage that results from his pursuit of a dream, from the unworthiness of the god to which he has dedicated his life and to which he, too, will finally sacrifice himself.

But the very happiness he invokes in his created past serves to underscore the gap between such images and his own sense of insufficiency and despair. He summons into existence a brother who is an embodiment of his own needs and ambitions, who will retrospectively validate past decisions no less than his present plan to ride to glory, but whose very existence is, in his own mind, a measure of his failure. He gradually loses control of the past as he has of the present, darker memories beginning to seep through. And where is Willy all this time, his mind flooded with memories of the past, his eyes still bright with visions of a possible future? He feels "kind of temporary;" in other words he feels effectively outside of time, caught between a suspect past and an ever-receding future.

Time is the needle that sews the sampler that is *Death of a Salesman*, and time does strange things in that play as in the first minutes we leap, via the sound of a flute, from the late 19th century to the 1940s and then the 1920s; but that is because Willy Loman is a time traveller. Past and future are as substantial as the present within which, nonetheless, they are both compacted. In one sense the events of the play take place over a period of twenty four hours. In another sense, as Miller suggests, they take place over some two and a half hours. In yet another sense the time period is nearly sixty years.

But Miller has also talked of the "social time" of the play and of its "psychic time," in other words, the social setting, with its assumptions about private morality and public actions, and the special time created by the tumble of memories which form an interference pattern with Willy's daily life. Time is curiously plastic and multi-layered in *Salesman,* a fact which sets directors and designers significant challenges. And the effect of clashing time scales is to breed irony, expose causality, dissolve identity, imply responsibility, reveal emotional and spiritual debility, social change, psychological process. As Miller has said, "I wanted a way of presenting [time] so that it became the fiber of the play" (Martin 422). Perhaps not so much the fibre as the fibre optics, as light from one time and place suddenly floods into another. He wanted, in particular, to turn the diachronic into the synchronic, cutting down through time "like a cake." And, indeed, past and present do exist within the same moment in this play. Why? Because "everything we are is at every moment alive in us" (*Timebends* 131).

His aim, then, was to capture "the mind's simultaneity," to enable Willy Loman "to see present through past and past through present" (*Timebends* 131). Although Ibsen is thought of as an influence behind *All My Sons* rather than *Salesman*, what he saw in Ibsen is equally applicable to this story of an aging salesman caught in a time warp, re-experiencing the past, not as memory, but as present fact. In Ibsen, Miller has said, "Past and present were drawn in to a single continuity" so that as a consequence "a secret moral order was...limned," an order in which "present dilemma was simply the face that the past had left visible." For Miller, indeed, "A play without a past is a mere shadow of a play" (McFarlane 229-30).

But there are other kinds of time in *Death of a Salesman*. Willy Loman is mesmerised by a national myth embodied in the person of his brother Ben who went into the jungle and came out rich. But, as Frank Kermode has said, "Myths take place in a quite different order of time." The only way to gain access to them "is by ritual re-enactment. But here and now, in *hoc tempore* (in this time], we are certain only of the dismal linearity of time" (Gray 272). That is the special dilemma of Willy Loman, as myth comes into conflict with the quotidian. He desperately wishes to re-enact the rituals which will revalidate the myth, the myth which operates in a quite different order of time, but is trapped in the desperate logic of linearity. He engages in ritual actions—setting out on the road to his future, sowing seeds for a fruitful tomorrow—but these are gestures without meaning, without consequence. He summons Ben as evidence of the myth, but linear time, for this sixty-three year old man, will not relent.

The link between myth and language is metaphor. It is Willy Loman's fate, therefore, to be trapped in a metaphor, that of a tantalising dream, the American dream for which identity, meaning, epiphany are a product of tomorrow.

Then there is another kind of time that Miller sees as bearing on this play about a salesman who travels in the belief that a journey implies a destination, who shadows his pioneer father who headed west before the frontier was closed, selling what he made. This has to do with making as well as selling, the time measured by how long it takes to write a play or make a piece of furniture. Willy's father labour. He has nothing more to sell than himself. For Miller, the break between making and selling "has terrible consequences." As he has said:

> There are so many elements in things that a man or woman makes that you never even think about. The whole question of time is different. A man who is, say, a good carpenter will look at a job and immediately has got to think how long this is going to take...it is congealed time and what the machine has done is, in effect, to destroy that element of the human mind for a lot of people. They no longer respect the time that is in objects...human time. They lose contact with reality, which is also the question of the rolling away of your life, in terms of its minutes and seconds and hours. It is terribly important.

To make something, then, is to retain a grasp on the real, to maintain a sense of "human time" and hence of "mortality" and thus ultimate values. Willy Loman has lost that. He no longer makes things, though we are told that he was never so much himself as when he did, briefly, do so. But now he inhabits a world in which such things no longer seem to have true significance. Human time, the time locked up in a piece of furniture or a front stoop, has deferred to something else. Now, time is measured by how long it takes a refrigerator belt to fail or a car to break down or a salesman to sell a product that is so detached from him that he never refers to it.

This concern is there, too, incidentally, in *The Last Yankee*, in which a wife upbraids her carpenter husband for not putting his skills at the service of success. But he is a craftsman. There is time invested in the work he does, as there is in the life of a man or woman. And there is a line to be traced from there to *Mr. Peters' Connections*, for Miller has said that once people have lost touch with the human time embodied in the objects they make, they, in turn, "get disembodied"—like Mr. Peters—and lose contact with reality. And once the connection between making and doing has gone, once a fundamental awareness of that congealed human time has disappeared, what is left appears to be no more than passing time or, more significantly, killing time. Instead of living our lives, we are, Miller suggests, now "living other people's lives," and the mechanism for that is television, which, he laments, in this country, "is all night and all day." For Mr. Peters, his is a country that has lost "is all night and all day." For Mr. Peters, his is a country that has lost the plot, its subject. It is no longer Willy Loman who feels "kind of temporary" but the whole culture as buildings are torn down and rebuilt, businesses disappear, history itself becomes disposable (an echo here of the lament in *The Price* that now everything is disposable), and, on television, programme succeeds programme with no logic, inner coherence or connection with individual lives.

In *Death of a Salesman,* the failing machines have their parallel in a failing man. Willy's boss, Howard, no longer recognises the human time locked up in this aging salesman, a man who enters his office to insist on the moral authority of the past, on a contract once made, an obligation once acknowledged. But Howard's values are those of business. He is a man for whom time is money, who has no time for the man who has served the company for most of his life and has little time left. Ultimately, of course, Willy's only means of stopping time is to stop himself, as Eddie Carbone, who had tried to stop the biological clock by denying his niece's sexual maturity, in order to deny the reality of his own sexual feelings towards her, can finally only retain his own innocence by stopping the clock of his own life.

The past, actual, distorted, re-invented, is crucial to Miller's work. It is hard to think of a Miller play in which it does not rest heavily on the present. It is fundamental to his belief in causality and moral responsibility. His repeated reminder that his plays—like those of classical Greece and Ibsen—are about the chickens coming home to roost merely underscores a truth evident from *The Golden Years* through to *Mr. Peters' Connections.* The denial, of which so many of his characters are guilty, is in essence a denial of the past and of its secrets. And since the denial of the past is necessarily a denial of the self, of an identity that is a product of the past, no wonder his characters tend to shout out their names when they are in process of denying the identity with which they like to believe they have invested those names. A denial of the past is, in effect, a denial of identity and of reality.

Yet the past, as we have seen, is not hard-edged, verifiable, agreed. As a character says in *The Creation of the World and Other Business,* "The past is always changing." It is a field of contention. And since memory exists not in the past but the present, there is a temporal distortion as that past is made to serve current needs. As Miller has said of Willy Loman, his "attitude to the past is always romantic...his brain embellishes everything. For Charley, what is real is real." That is, perhaps, Charley's redemption and his limitation. For Willy, past and future alike are golden. Only the present throws back no glow. It is that fact that simultaneously corrupts his present with irony and suggests a longing for transcendence and transformation that distinguishes him from Charley's realism, a realism whose limitation is signalled by his reply to Willy's accusation that he never took an interest in his son, Bernard: "My salvation is that I never took an interest in anything" (72). Willy has a passionate interest, fired by a disturbing amalgam of hope, need, guilt and love, by a desire to understand why his life is as it is. Willy has the writer's desire to charge the world with significance.

In *The Price*, too, a play in which the past has an objective correlative in the form of a roomful of furniture, differing versions of the past become the arena in which two brothers seek to justify their lives. In *Some Kind of Love Story*, the past is deeply problematic, a kind of holodeck in which two people locate themselves within competing narratives, while desperate for some connection, perhaps no longer between one and another but between themselves and their lives, between themselves and the real. And implicit in the question of memory is the question of reality. Without memory reality is literally deracinated, a series of gestures, events, feelings with no precursors, no cause, no form, no structure of meaning. But the reality of memories is itself, as we have seen, suspect. The past, then, is not secure in these plays. Things happen—betrayals of one kind or another—but the meaning of these things, the motives that generated them, is less so. There are few Miller characters for whom the past is unambiguous. It contains too many secrets, the seeds of too much guilt. All wish to declare their innocence but how can that innocence be assured if the past is granted true authority. They want to exist outside of time but, as Miller insists in *The Creation of the World and Other Business*, we exist, in the words of another play, after the fall. It was, after all, the fall of man that started the clock of history, that started the biological clock which numbered our days, that introduced time and with it causality and death.

Memory and consciousness are directly related. Even to understand this sentence you have to remember its beginning. In like manner, to understand a life you have to understand in what it has consisted. For William James, in *The Principles of Psychology*, that primary memory is to be distinguished from what he called secondary memory—"the rearward portion of the present space of time" (Parkin 2). The past is not the trailing edge of the present: but it is part of our present. We contain it. And that is why Quentin, in *After the Fall*, insists that the past is holy, for there is a price to be paid for denying it. It is a price paid by Joe Keller, by Willy Loman and, arguably, by the culture of which they are defining symbols. In Miller's plays we are taken back to that past through the wormhole which is memory, which is history, but which is also the theatre itself, surely the supreme time-machine with the power to transport us at warp-speed to that singularity which is the space between the mind and what it imagines, that space within which Miller's plays, indeed, arguably, all plays have their being.

Works Cited

Bigsby, Christopher. Interview with Arthur Miller, January 3, 1999. All unsourced references are to this or other such interviews.

Eliot, T.S. *The Selected Prose of T.S.Eliot*. London, 1975.

Faulkner, William. *Requiem for a Nun*. Harmondsworth, 1960.

Fowles, John. *Wormholes*. London, 1998.

Gray, Richard. *Writing the South*. Cambridge, 1986.

Hawthorne, Nathaniel. *The Scarlet Letter*. London, 1992.

Lippman, Amy. "Rhythm and Truths." *American Theatre*. April, 1984.

Martin, Robert A. and Steven R. Centola, *The Theater Essays of Arthur Miller*. New York: DaCapo Press, 1996.

McFarlane, James, ed. "Ibsen and the Drama of Today" in *The Cambridge Companion to Ibsen*. Cambridge, 1994.

Miller, Arthur. *The American Clock*. London, 1983.

---. *The Creation of the World and Other Business*. New York, 1973.

---. *Death of a Salesman*. New York: Penguin, 1999.

---. *Death of a Salesman* notebook. Harry Ransome Center, University of Texas.

---. "On Broadway: Notes on the Past and Future of the American Theatre." *Harper's Magazine*. March, 1999.

---. "Preface," *Death of a Salesman*, 50th Anniversary Edition. New York: Penguin, 1999.

---. *Timebends*. London: Grove Press, 1987.

Morse, Jonathan. *Word by Word: The Language of Memory*. Ithaca, 1990.

Parkin, Alan J. *Memory, Phenomena, Experiment, and Theory.* Oxford, 1993.

Terkel, Studs. *Hard Times: An Oral History of the Great Depression.* New York, 1970.

Celebrating *Salesman*

Matthew Roudané

The theater inhabits that relatively narrow space between the real and the imaginary. As Michal Kobialka argues in *Of Borders and Thresholds: Theatre History, Practice, and Theory* (1999), the theater is full of borders and boundaries:

> The separation between life and the imitation of life on stage, between the 'real' and the 'illusionary' conditions of the stage, between the way one functions in everyday life and the way one acts on stage, or between the words one hears and the text one reads, has always been at the very center of any discussion concerning one of the most fundamental questions in theatre studies—what it means to represent (4).

As such, the theater in general, and Miller's *Death of a Salesman* in particular, offer unique opportunities to examine the construction, representation, and functioning of many forms of borders or thresholds. Miller presents a Willy Loman who inhabits an ambiguous border, that interstice between Ibsen's vital lie and the unidealized reality of his depleted circumstances—

when "the woods are burning." Once a consummate, or at least competent, performer in his own life, Willy by play's end hasn't a story left in him to tell. *Salesman* gains much of its mimetic and cultural power precisely from Miller's interweaving the real with the imaginary. Whether crossing the white line of the highway or standing at the grave's edge, its characters always find themselves on a border, a threshold.

One challenge Miller posed for himself when he began writing plays during the 1930s and 40s was how to reconnoiter such borders. He was searching for a way to stage a compelling narrative in a new and engaging form. As Miller reflects in "Notes on the Past and Future of American Theater," which appeared in the March 1999 issue of *Harper's*, "When I began writing plays in the late Thirties, 'realism' was the reigning style in the English-language commercial theater, which was just about all the theater there was at the time in America and Britain" (38). Later in the essay Miller elaborates:

> My own first playwriting attempt was purely mimetic, a realistic play about my own family. It won me some prizes and productions, but, interestingly, I could not wait to turn at once to a stylized treatment of life in a gigantic prison—modeled on Jackson state penitentiary in Michigan, near Ann Arbor, where I was in school (42).

While his fellow unknown playwright of the 1930s was also composing his own play about a prison experience—*Not About Nightingale*—Miller found that in his new play about prison, *The Great Disobedience*, realistic language "could not engage so vast a human disaster with speech born in a warm kitchen" (42). Miller searched for a new language for the modern stage: "Was it possible," Miller wrote last month, "to create a style that would at once deeply engage an American audience that insisted on a recognizable reality of characters, locales, and themes while at the same time opening the stage to considerations of public morality and the mythic social fates—in short, to the invisible?" (42) It was for Miller, of course, very possible. Possible precisely because his new poetic language and innovative structures inhabited borders, thresholds: between Willy's not being able to pay the insurance—and yet paying off the mortgage the very day he dies; between boys built being like Adonises who project a hopeful future—yet who only turn into a philandering bum and a aimless drifter; between a Linda who knows all along that her husband is trying to kill himself and a wife who knows that she cannot do anything to prevent his suicide; and between a Willy who yearns for what's best for his boys but who leaves his sons fatherless. Even the title of this essay, "Celebrating *Salesman*," suggests something of the border, the intersection of conflicting emotions inscribed in Miller's play: we stood last night applauding, weeping, and celebrating a death-saturated play about a family largely unwilling to "face facts" and whose antihero is a fated "salesman with his feet on the subway stairs and his head in the stars" (xi), to use Miller's words from the new preface to the 50th anniversary edition of the play.

Miller instinctively knew about the intrinsic power imbedded in dramatic borders. Listen to what he explains, again from the new preface:

> *All My Sons* had all but convinced me that if one totally integrated a play's conceptual life with its emotional one so that there was no perceptible *dividing line between the two* (my emphasis), such a play could reach such an audience [a mainstream Broadway audience unreceptive to serious plays staged in challenging forms]. In short, they had to move forward not by following a narrow, discreet line, but as a phalanx, all of its elements moving together simultaneously. There was no model I could adopt for this play, no past history for the kind of work I felt it could become. What I had before me was the way the mind—at least my mind—actually worked. One asks a policeman for directions; as one listens, the hairs sticking out of his nose become important, reminding one of a father, brother, son with the same feature, and one's conflicts with him or one's friendship come to mind, and all this over a period of seconds while objectively taking note of how to get to where one wants to go. . . .Willy rapidly took over my imagination and became something that had never existed before, a salesman with his feet on the subway stairs and his head in the stars (xi).

In brief, Miller wanted to break from realistic boundaries and to stage a play imbued with a moral seriousness and social complexity in a wholly new form. He created nothing less than a new poetics. The notion of creating a sense of simultaneity, a dramatic process by which he could bend time, became increasingly important. Miller felt that the "problem with *All My Sons* was not that it was too realistic but that it left too little space and time for the wordless darkness that underlies all verbal truth" (*Timebends*, 144). For *Salesman,* photographic realism simply could not reflect the interior subjectivity he was seeking. He needed a form and a language that exteriorized the conflated borders of Willy's imagination, and the result was, of course, a play that revolutionized the ontological status of the theater, that transfigured its very borders, its very essence. Its universality, despite what some postmodernists who say otherwise, seems undeniable. As Miller claims in the new preface, "This play seems to have shown that most of the world shares something similar to" the plight of the Lomans. Audiences viewing the play from around the world, Miller has stated for years, find themselves on similar familial borders, similar professional thresholds, and similar psychological precipices. As Miller wrote in February of this year, *Salesman* maps out familial and familiar turf: "namely that being human—a father, mother, son—is something most of us fail at most of the time, and a little mercy is eminently in order given the societies we live in, which purport to be stable and sound as mountains when in fact they are all trembling in a fast wind blowing mindlessly around the earth" (xii-xiii). Stable and sound, yet trebling in a fast wind, blowing mindlessly around our global border, the earth itself.

It is hardly surprising, then, to see that Willy is consigned to problematic existence. Although Miller has said that his 1949 play was set in the 1930s, he also really felt that its social time was in the 1920s. If we bring a certain elasticity to our definitions of time—as Miller and his famed antihero do—we see that Willy, despite the modernity of his situation, is as much a product of the nineteenth century as he is of the twentieth. Born a generation after Melville's confidence men inhabited America and essentially a child of Twain's Gilded Age, Willy comes of age when Dreiser's Sister Carrie was drawn to an acting career in New York City. Symbolically enough, Willy was in his hey day as a salesman in the roaring Twenties. Or at least he claimed to have earned $128 a week the very year O'Neill staged the appropriately entitled *Strange Interlude*. But despite growing up as a boy in the late nineteenth-century America in which robber barons made notions of democracy largely a lie of the mind, despite fathering one child at the start of World War I and the second at the end of World War I, despite maturing as a salesman in the roaring Twenties when the Jay Gatsbys of the country were bankrolling millions, and despite his idolization of Dave Singleman, Willy's life clearly intersected with the Great Depression and obviously extends to the actual time of the play itself at mid-century. Whatever models of entrepreneurship and community he bought into, the contemporary sixty-three year old Willy of the play is now ill-equipped to deal with Howard's world, the world animated by a "business is business" vocabulary and such newfangled, thoroughly postmodern inventions as the baffling tape recorder. He is a salesman no longer capable of selling, a fatherless father incapable of recognizing the love around him. For audiences today, Willy Loman's name has become part of a national vocabulary, an instantly recognizable name synonymous with Every Person's struggle to cross borders—from being nameless, an insignificant speck in the universe over which we have little or no control, to leaving one's thumbprint on the world. He must constantly name and re-name himself. Forever doomed to linger in the margins, Willy locates himself in the epicenter of a public world: "Go to Slattery's, Boston. Call out the name Willy Loman and see what happens! Big shot!" As such, *Salesman* has become at least as much if not more resonate for 1999 as for 1949 audiences.

So I admit to being slightly taken aback when the Chief Cultural Critic for the *Los Angeles Times,* who called me in January to talk about a feature article he was preparing on the play, challenged my thoughts about the play's relevance and resonance to 1999 audiences. Wasn't the play somehow dated? Don't members of the audience know today that putting three decades into a firm, and the sense of loyalty that goes with such longevity, no longer squares with the reality of the market place? "Aren't the young now instructed that they will have several careers?" he asked (cf. Liberman). On the one hand, of course, Mr. Liberman was right: visiting the world of the Lomans does seem like a trip down memory lane when compared to the world of Mamet's salesman, Shepard's splintered families, or Kushner's anguished figures.

The Lomans are clearly inhabitants of another, distant, and simpler era. One the other hand, it seems clear that we celebrate *Salesman* a half a century later because it is even more resonate, more reflective of what Shakespeare called that magic charm of the theater.

Death of a Salesman presents a matrix of enabling fables that define the myth of the American dream. Indeed, most theatergoers assume that the principles Willy Loman values—initiative, hard work, family, freedom, consumerism, economic salvation, competition, the frontier, self-sufficiency, public recognition, personal fulfillment, and so on—animate American cultural poetics. The Founding Fathers, after all, predicated the U. S. Constitution on the belief that every citizen possesses the inalienable right to the unfettered pursuit of the American Dream. No wonder Benjamin Franklin's practical 1757 essay on how to achieve Salvation, *The Way to Wealth* (whose title would have prompted Willy Loman to buy a copy), attracted the common working person. Although Willy Loman, inspired by a mythologized Dave Singleman and a desire to build a future for his boys through hard work, endorses such values, it is an endorsement foisted upon him less by personal choice than by a malevolent universe whose hostility mocks his every pursuit. Well-meaning yet lacking, a fatherless father, a salesman no longer capable of selling, Willy Loman can only cling to idyllic fables that baffle as they elude him.

Death of a Salesman replicates a model of community and of citizenship to which most theatergoers—regardless of gender, race, nationality, or ideology—respond. The nature of that popular and intellectual response varies greatly, to be sure. The play embodies, for many, the hubris that Aristotle found essential for all great tragedies. For many feminist critics, on the other hand, the play stages a grammar of space that marginalizes Linda Loman and, by extension, all women, who seem Othered, banished to the periphery of a patriarchal world. *Death of a Salesman*, the universalists counter, seems beyond philosophical limits or gendered subjectivity, and thus is a play to which all—social constructionists, Jungians, Marxists, poststructuralists, and so on—react.

Such praise comes from the notion that most in the audience relate to as they rebel against the Lomans. The adulterous father.

The marginalized mother. Wayward children. A family's battles to pay bills. Unemployment. The child's quest. Spite. Loss. Felt but unexpressed love. Guilt and shame. Self-reliance. Theatergoers see themselves, their parents, or their children in the play. A play concerning the most public of American myths, *Death of a Salesman* lays bare the private individual's sensibility, a sensibility neutralized by those very myths. In an era when many scholars question precisely what constitutes American essentialism, most theatergoers still regard *Death of a Salesman* as the quintessential American play. But the play also transcends its own borders, its American heritage and claims to American essentialism.

The play continues to engage audiences on an international level, not only because it traverses intercultural borders, but also because it brings audiences back to the edges of prehistory itself. Postmodern in texture, reifying a world in which experience is "always already" for the Lomans, the play gains its theatrical power from ancient echoes, its Hellenic mixture of pity and fear stirring primal emotions. Miller himself has stated for a half a century that because the play embeds within its innovative structure certain primal experiences, audiences around the world respond intellectually and emotionally to the play. Audiences respond because, despite the play's modernity, tribal undercurrents animate the narrative. Perhaps this is why, for many, *Death of a Salesman* remains the quintessential American play, while *The Crucible* occupies a central place in any narrative history of American drama. His strong work of the 1990s are dramas whose scripts indicate that Miller has maintained control over his mimetic powers. A playwright born on the eve of World War I, who came of age during the Great Depression, was a major force in postwar theater and remains a significant force as we near the twenty-first century, Arthur Miller may rightfully be regarded as one of America's most inventive and exemplary artists.

Despite the diminished world of the Lomans, and despite the threat of apocalypse in *After the Fall, Incident at Vichy, Playing for Time,* and in *Broken Glass,* Miller provides a resolution of sorts throughout his theater. This resolution may be best understood in the context of the playwright's intellectual position, which reveals itself through his moral optimism. From *The Golden Years* through *Broken Glass,* Miller emphasizes the primacy of the individual's social duty and the importance of familial love. Implicit in all the major plays is Miller's belief in the unifying force of love that creates the possibility for social revolt in the polis and personal insight within the family. These essentializing forces, which elude the Lomans and which leave the Proctor children without a father, only increase the tragic force of Miller's cosmology. The poetics of Arthur Miller are informed with a sense of charity and love which the Lomans can never adequately express. This is why Linda Loman, sobbing quietly as the lights fade, can only contemplate what could, or should, have been. In *Broken Glass*, Sylvia attempts to name her emotional and physical paralysis, but she is unable to articulate its sources or identify its etiology. But, through Miller's moral optimism, it's also why at the final curtain Sylvia Gellburg can stand, taking her first steps toward a recovery of more than a physical kind. A playwright of an older generation, Arthur Miller remains a timeless pioneer who keeps his, and the audience's, eye on the future.

In sum, Miller's theater is at its best when inhabiting the space between the real and the imaginary. Such "in-betweenness" gives the plays its unique theatricality. His is a theater filled with borders, thresholds. In 1995, Miller observed to what extent any truly great play crosses thresholds and borders: ". . . what a tremendous door out into the universe the theatre can be" (*80th Birthday*, n.p.). *Death of a Salesman, The Crucible,* and the other great Miller plays give audiences and actors alike such a door, an entrance to a transcendent experience. This is why his are characters who haven't "played" for time, but who are—and I emphasize the presentness of the present—who are playing for the precious moments of their lives, trying, as in his most recent play, to make connections, traversing borders whenever possible or whenever unavoidable. Somehow it was fitting, then, to see the playwright honored in 1999 with a street named after him— *Arthur Miller Way.* It is most appropriate because it, and Miller himself, lie at the intersection, the border, the crossroad of American theater itself.

Works Cited

Kobialka, Michal. "Introduction: Of Borders and Thresholds," in Kobialka, ed. *Of Borders and Thresholds: Theatre History, Practice, and Theory.* Minneapolis: U Minnesota P, 1999 , 1-29.

Liberman, Paul. "Miller's Undying 'Salesman.'" *Los Angeles Times,* February 5, 1999, A-1, A-8-9.

Miller, Arthur. "Notes on the Past and Future of American Theatre." *Harper's Magazine,* March 1999, 38-42.

---. "Preface: *Salesman* At Fifty." In *Death of a Salesman.* 50th Anniversary Edition, New York: Penguin, 1999, ix-xiii.

---. *Timebends: A Life.* New York: Grove, 1987.

---. *Arthur Miller: 80th Birthday.* Arthur Miller Center, 1995.

The 1999 Revival of *Death of a Salesman*

A Critical Commentary

Brenda Murphy

The 1999 New York revival of *Death of a Salesman* originated at the Goodman Theater in Chicago, where it opened on September 28, 1998, and subsequently moved to Broadway, where it opened on February 10, 1999, fifty years to the day after the play's original New York premiere. The production was directed by Robert Falls, and featured Brian Dennehy and Elizabeth Franz as Willy and Linda Loman. All three of them won Tony Awards, in addition to a Tony for the Season's best revival. The cast also included Kevin Anderson as Biff, Ted Koch as Happy, and Howard Witt as Charley. Anderson and Witt were nominated for Tonys. The set design was by Mark Wendland, the lighting by Michael Philippi, the music and sound by Richard Woodbury. The New York producer was David Richenthal.

This successful and highly praised production sparked a new interest in *Salesman,* and, as the Dustin Hoffman production had done in 1984, presented a new interpretation of the play for a new generation. What follows is a commentary on the interpretive issues arising from the revival, many of which were first raised in reviews and critical discussions of the production. This review will begin with the larger interpretive and conceptual questions and end with the particulars of performance.

The Director's Interpretation

In the criticism following its first production in 1949, *Death of a Salesman* was both praised and damned for its politics.[1] While Miller has written that "a play cannot be equated with a political philosophy" (*Theater* 150), he has also written that "Willy Loman has broken a law without whose protection life is insupportable if not incomprehensible to him and to many others; it is the law which says that a failure in society and business has no right to live" (*Theater* 149). No one who encounters the play can fail to miss its critique of the capitalist system. A given production, however, may choose to de-emphasize its political thematics in order to emphasize other thematic implications. Many critics have suggested that this is the case with the Falls production. A compelling description of Robert Falls's overall concept for the production was given by Ben Brantley, whose *New York Times* piece on the Goodman production was a large factor in bringing it to New York. He wrote that: "Darkness is the primary element of director Robert Falls's exquisitely reimagined staging" of the play:

> Darkness is always waiting for Willy Loman. It laps away at the edges of even his sunniest memories. It clouds his vision to the point that he cannot trust himself to drive. It keeps pulling him back, with gravitational force, whenever hopes, however small, are rekindled. The darkness terrifies Willy. You can sense that in the lost, panicked expression that abruptly takes over his face. But there is never any doubt that he is going to surrender to it (3 Nov. 1998).

A consistent theme in the critical response to the production has been that it is centered on the personal—the family and its dynamics, the psychology of Willy's breakdown—downplaying if not ignoring its socio-political meaning. Brantley wrote that "Mr. Falls and his fiercely engaged cast are, above all, committed to the work's tragic, conflicted familial love story, between husband and wife, between father and sons" (11 Feb.). Lloyd Rose wrote in the *Washington Post* that "Director Robert Falls has decided to focus on Biff's story." "This is the play about hating your father and loving your father and owing your father and, above all, never being good enough for your father. About letting the old man down." David Klinghoffer praised the production in the conservative *National Review*, no great friend to Miller's work or ideas, by saying that "the play works agonizingly well. Not as any type of socialist harangue, but rather as a meditation on manhood." Mainstream journalists also expressed approval of what they saw as the production's emphasis of family relationships and downplaying its politics. *USA Today* said that:

> Director Robert Falls introduces some subtle revisionism: There's nothing wrong with the American dream, only with those, like Willy Loman, who are naive enough to think it will come to them . . . thus, his wife's famous 'attention must be paid' speech is less a socialist tract than a sermon on unconditional love: Just because Loman was low on the capitalist food chain doesn't mean he's less of a person" (Stearns).

Robert Feldberg suggested in the *Bergen Record* that, "by focusing so intensely on Willy, [Falls] makes it clear that, at bottom, the play is about a man's relationship with his family, and that it wasn't the American dream that curdled Willy's life but his twisted view of it."

In this context, it is worthwhile to remember Arthur Miller's comments in his 1956 essay, "The Family in Modern Drama." All plays that we call serious, he wrote, are ultimately concerned with some aspect of a single problem:

> How may a man make of the outside world a home?" If "the struggle in *Death of a Salesman* were simply between father and son for recognition and forgiveness it would diminish in importance. But when it extends itself out of the family circle and into society, it broaches those questions of social status, social honor and recognition, which expand its vision and lift it out of the merely particular toward the fate of the generality of men (*Theater* 73-74).

Jack Helbig demonstrated Miller's idea in his discussion of the father-son relationship as central to Falls's interpretation:

> Falls reveals a much larger pattern at work in the play by emphasizing how Willy Loman is part of an intergenerational rat race he cannot leave. Loman never felt loved by his father and always

felt, in his word, 'temporary' about himself. So he threw himself into his brutal salesman's life on the road, never got to really know his sons—Happy is especially neglected—so they in turn feel temporary about themselves. At the play's end, Loman's son, Happy, steps onto the treadmill, clearly hoping, as his father foolishly hoped, that hard work alone would redeem him.

What Robert Falls has done is to make the family the locus of social conflict and also a synecdochic figure for the larger society. He records the devastation that is wreaked upon the individual and the family, leaving the audience to contemplate its implications for "the generality of men." The power of this dramatic figuration has been great enough to impel many critics and spectators to think beyond the particular, but Falls's approach has also allowed some to take refuge in it.

The Design Concept

The Jo Mielziner design for the original set of *Death of a Salesman* is legendary. It fixed the style of subjective realism that he had been developing in Tennessee Williams's *The Glass Menagerie* (1944) and *A Streetcar Named Desire* (1947), and it solved the dilemma that Miller had presented for the designer, in desiring a physical representation of Willy Loman's way of mind at that "terrible moment when the voice of the past is no longer distant but quite as loud as the voice of the present" (Miller, *Theater* 138), suggesting the "mobile concurrency of past and present. . .because in his desperation to justify his life Willy Loman has destroyed the boundaries between now and then" (138-39). Mielziner's solution might be seen as modernist in approach. His central design concept was the constant presence of the Loman's house on the stage, the objective correlative, as he saw it, for the American Dream. The expressionist elements of his design, the crucial lighting changes that signified the subjective shifts in Willy's consciousness, worked in juxtaposition with this material signifier of the Salesman's dream. Mielziner's house was a constant reminder of a cultural myth that once provided a sense of purpose for Americans like Willy Loman. The subjective reality surrounding it—threatening, unstable, constantly shifting—suggested the disintegration of the myth in the nation's consciousness.

Mielziner's design suggested the modernist's perception that his accepted verities and institutions and myths are fragmenting and falling away, but also the modernist's desire to somehow find an aesthetic way to make them whole again, an art that will provide the integration that the culture has lost.

At least one critic has suggested that, in relation to Mielziner's, Mark Wendland's approach to the design is post-modern rather than modernist. Chris Jones wrote that "with a drastically post-modern concept that explodes those familiar Jo Mielziner images of the Willy Loman home into a disconnected and alienated series of floating boxes and pieces, Falls and designer Mark Wendland breathed vibrant new energy into the play by releasing it from the shackles of domestic design of modified realism." On the other hand, John Istel asserted that "Wendland has not so much deconstructed Loman's elemental American home as dissected and redefined Mielziner's initial impulse."

I would like to go into some detail in suggesting that Wendland has in fact deconstructed the Mielziner design, exchanging the post-modernist aesthetic for the modernist. While he makes use of some of Mielziner's techniques, he has given up the modernist yearning for the integrated myths of the past represented by the house in favor of a frank representation of the fragmentation of the American family and its myths. His design for the Loman's house is a representation of the instability of both the Loman family and their dreams.

The opening burst of bright light that outlines the massive body of Brian Dennehy and the enormous burden of his sample cases in the frame of the door, "like a man-mountain action hero on a final mission," as Linda Winer has put it, is a post-modern gesture that momentarily acknowledges the character's status as cultural icon, and that does not fail to register with the audience. After the initial shock of the bank of floodlights that emphasize Willy's return, Michael Philippi's overall lighting concept takes over. The minimal set begins very dark, with blue light filtered through a Venetian blind pattern. Ben Brantley has suggested that it creates "a sense of engulfing night that evokes William Styron's notion of emotional depression as 'darkness visible.'" (3 Nov.). In the opening sequences, the set changes are achieved solely by means of revolving platforms: the parents' bed revolves upstage as the boys on their twin beds revolve down; the kitchen furniture revolves downstage during the daydream scene. This fragmentation of the house, the abstract minimalism in establishing the set, and the parallel but unintegrated action by the characters establishes the disintegration of the Loman family visually as well as solving the problem of immediate scene changes from the kitchen to the parents' bedroom to the boys' bedroom that Mielziner had solved through his single set and lighting design.

During the first daydream scene, the theatrical idiom that will define the performance is filled out. At stage right appears the double box set, which includes the kitchen upstage, lighted during this scene, and the Lomans' bedroom downstage, dark during this scene. Significantly, the space of the kitchen is fragmented during this scene. The chairs and table revolve to downstage left, at the opposite end of the stage from the box set, for most of the scene. For Linda's scene with the boys, the kitchen's box set is moved to center stage, and the table and chairs in front of it, a temporarily integrated image of the kitchen with a bright, amber light shining on the table for this momentary glimpse of the Lomans' attempt to confront the reality of Willy's situation together. This image of family is extended momentarily to include Willy, as the family sits at the table discussing the Oliver deal, but is broken up as Biff confronts Willy over "yelling at" Linda and the temporary reconstruction of the Loman family disintegrates.

For the last scene of act 1, Willy and Linda are enclosed in the box set of their bedroom while the boys stand downstage, outside of the box, to say goodnight, a scenic representation of their dissociation from their parents that is further heightened when Biff walks toward the center of the stage and stands facing the audience and smoking a cigarette as Willy talks to Linda about his football glory, and then goes through the basement door to bring up the rubber pipe that signifies Willy's suicidal state, which he carries "upstairs" to the roof of the kitchen box set to end the act. In these scenes, Wendland's kitchen and bedroom boxes resonate both security and confinement, the attempt to recapture and retain both the family's structure and its myths of the past. Falls's placement of the boys in relation to the boxes suggests both their attraction and their resistance to it.

For the kitchen scene in act 2, when the boys return from the restaurant, the kitchen is again fragmented. Only the kitchen table and chairs are used for the confrontational scene between Linda and the boys, and the perspective is further split as Biff looks out at the audience while he speaks of watching Willy, who can be seen upstage. Willy is then revolved to the center and the table revolves upstage. This is the last we see of the kitchen's box set, as Biff sets about taking apart the last of the Loman family myths and Willy's mind disintegrates into self-destruction.

Wendland's design solution for the transition from past to present in the first daydream scene combines some of Mielziner's techniques with his own post-modern ones. The leaf projections that Mielziner used as a scenic environment to signify Willy's subjective shift into the past are foregrounded as an aesthetic device by Wendland. Willy sits at the table in semi-darkness, talking about the car. The leaf-projections come up as translucent screens are moved to the sides and the light is brought up on "the back yard." The leaf projections appear on a large screen over the stage, a post-modern framing device that causes the projection to resonate as symbol rather than an expressionistic attempt to represent a subjective environment as it was by Mielziner. Similarly, Wendland places the red Chevy, an objective correlative for Willy's romanticized idyllic relationship with the boys, in a central position upstage, although it is used only briefly at the beginning of the scene.

The overall effect of the design scheme is to treat Mielziner's original design for the play as an artifact, to emphasize its existence as art by "quoting" it, and at the same time to emphasize its nature as an artistic construction by taking it apart and examining the parts. At the same time, Wendland's fragmentation of the set and the symbol of the house helps to convey a sense of the family as more hopelessly fragmented than the original design did. The Lomans in the original production had the house, the symbol of their lost integrity as a family, always in the background as a reminder of their yearnings. The Lomans in the revival, like the set, come together only momentarily in family configurations, which suggest nostalgic traces of a lost family structure rather than a lost ideal they are striving to regain.

Music

The original production of *Death of a Salesman* opened with the familiar, haunting flute melody composed by Alex North, which began 5 counts after the house lights went out and continued until Willy's line, "I'm tired to the death," creating a subtext or accompaniment "telling of grass and trees and the horizon," as Miller was to write in the published play (11). The Falls production opens with car sounds as the lights fade. There is no flute at all, a controversial aspect of the production. Richard Woodbury's score combines loud drums and trumpets, rising in a crescendo to a "jungle beat" of drums, in which the music becomes an environment of Darwinian menace rather than the nostalgic accompaniment it was in the original. It is resolved into a single theme played on a trumpet. The music throughout suggests a jazzy, urban subtext rather than the gentle pastoral that was used in the original production and that is suggested by Miller's published stage directions. The jazz theme provides the segue between Linda's phone call to Biff and the scene in Howard's office. The loud music is repeated in crescendo at the end of the play to suggest the suicide crash. It is the threat of the present, of the darkness engulfing Willy, that is suggested by this music, rather than the siren-like enticement of the past that is suggested in the Alex North score. It helps to emphasize the dark, fragmented, and threatening environment that Willy inhabits on stage, effacing the subtext of nostalgia that was suggested by the flute music and the lighting of the daydream scenes in the original production.

Acting

Given his imposing bulk, Brian Dennehy's Willy is necessarily in the tradition of the "Big Willys"—Lee J. Cobb and George C. Scott, for example—than that of the "Small Willys"—Dustin Hoffman, Hume Cronyn, Warren Mitchell. Dennehy's general concept for Willy in the context of Falls's production has been aptly described by Ben Brantley:

> The production plays hauntingly on the contrast between Mr. Dennehy's imposing frame and the sad, scared gestures of a sickly child. When Willy shields his face with his hands, palms outward, during an argument with his son Biff, the effect is devastating in a way it wouldn't be with a physically slighter actor. The image of a big man made small perfectly embodies the argument for *Salesman*

as a bona fide tragedy.

Several critics have suggested that Dennehy enacts clinical depression in a way that is terrifying in its naturalism. Brantley has written that "Mr. Dennehy's stunningly disciplined performance is also sure to set off tremors in anyone who has known depression or lived with someone who suffers from it. When Linda says 'a terrible thing is happening to him,' it doesn't seem like hyperbole. Just watch how he works himself up to a pitch of confident bluster and then deflates in a single instant, as though forced to remember that life has never kept its promises." Placing Dennehy's performance in the context of Falls's overall concept of the play, Edward Karam wrote in the London *Times* that:

> A form of infantilism is strikingly on display in Robert Falls's nightmarish, expressionistic 50th-anniversary production of *Death of a Salesman* . . . Falls links [the boys'] emotional immaturity to Brian Dennehy's burly, vulnerable Willy Loman, who has never adapted his adolescent dreams to reality . . . the production . . . makes more of the Lomans' psychological dysfunction than of the overfamiliar plight of workers discarded by society.

In an America Online interview, Dennehy said that "in two days of his life [Willy's] living through the manic depression of his life. Making those transitions believable is very demanding. It's tricky" (AOL CHAT). While most critics, and audiences, have found Dennehy's interpretation of Willy powerful and moving, there has been some objection to his approach. Lloyd Rose wrote that "the production's biggest weakness . . .is Dennehy's performance as Willy . . . .Dennehy's drawback as an actor is that he can't convince you he knows pain. . . .He can make Willy crazy, but he can't make us believe that he suffers."

The ethnicity of Willy Loman has been an object of comment in several productions, including the original, with the Jewish Lee J. Cobb eventually being replaced by the Irish Thomas Mitchell. Miller has been accused both of making the Lomans too Jewish in their speech patterns and of deracinating them in order to appeal to a wider audience.[2] I would like to suggest that in Dennehy's hands, Willy is not only a convincing salesman, but a specifically Irish one. When he tells the story of Dave Singleman to Howard, he shows the gift of Irish blarney that has gotten him through a career of thirty-four years with the Wagner firm. Howard is *interested* in the story, and Willy enjoys telling it until the desperation of his situation breaks through and he abruptly loses his confidence with the line "They don't know me any more" (81). In that exchange one can briefly see Willy's whole life on the road, and the camaraderie of the early days that he has found it so devastating to lose. In Dennehy's performance, one can see that while the roots of Miller's experience of salesman are in American Jewish culture, he has created a character who can be fully and powerfully realized in a number of American ethnic contexts.

The juxtaposition of the concept-driven post-modern staging with Dennehy's naturalistic, and very natural, approach to Willy suggests some interesting questions, such as the conception of character that is accommodated within this realm of performance and the desired response from the audience. The artists connected with the production have expressed great satisfaction with the audience's emotional response to the play. Clearly this is no Brechtian production. Yet the undermining of the mimetic illusion in the staging works effectively with the naturalistic acting style. The effect is to foreground the actors and their performances. Dennehy seems massive on the minimal stage, and the powerful emotions in the performances of Elizabeth Franz and Kevin Anderson are shown in sharp relief against its background.

One of the overwhelming critical reactions to the production has been the approval of Franz's interpretation of Linda. Richard Christiansen set the tone for the response when he wrote in the Chicago *Tribune* of the Goodman production:

> Franz. . .gives us more than the customary fragile saint. Here is a woman with steel in her spine and fire in her gut too, when the time comes to lash out at the injustices she sees falling on the man she loves. Her elemental rendition of the play's final shattering scene is totally, completely brilliant.

Chris Jones wrote of the Goodman production:

> In a role that often comes off as a shrewish enabler, Franz emphasizes Linda's own needs and gives this woman resonance in

the post-feminist age. In the play's final moments, Franz splays her body over her husband's grave—a striking image of the prices wives paid for the sins and limitations of their breadwinner husbands.

Arthur Miller said in an interview that Franz has "mounted a kind of wonderful outrage I've never quite seen before" (Applebome B27). There is a general assumption among the newspaper critics that Linda has always been portrayed as a helpless, passive character, and they have been surprised to find how powerful she is. Brantley wrote that "Ms. Franz's astonishing portrayal shatters that character's traditional passivity to create a searing image of a woman fighting for her life, for that is what Willy is to Linda . . . it is with a fury that scorches. If need be, she will sacrifice her children for her husband, to whom she clearly remains, on some level, sexually bonded" (11 Feb). Donald Lyons of the *New York Post* wrote that "Elizabeth Franz really takes a new look at Linda Loman, Willy's wife, who emerges not as a hand-wringing dishrag but a smart, sharp, sensible woman who has made a pained peace with the failings of her husband and insists that her sons do the same. Fragile and tremulous, this Linda is yet capable of blasts of anger and of joy."

It is interesting that the image of Linda as fragile saint or hand-wringing dishrag should be so pervasive, given that Mildred Dunnock's original portrayal of the role combined a hard-won toughness with a sense of fragility that was similar to Franz's. The original director, Elia Kazan, wrote in his notebook that Linda "has consciously made her peace with her fate. She has chosen Willy! To hell with every one else. She is terrifyingly tough. Why? She senses Willy is in danger. And she just can't have him hurt" (47). Kazan elicited the desired outrage from Dunnock in the "Attention must be paid" scene by making her repeat the speech over and over, while he stabbed a fencing foil at her and yelled, "You've got more and damn it, you'll give it to me! You're a tigress defending her cub! Now, attack that scene—again, again!" (Poling 58). There was plenty of outrage in Dunnock's performance, but not the sexuality that Franz has brought to the role.

Several critics have recognized the range and authenticity of Franz's performance, but seem trapped in the critical cliché that Arthur Miller cannot write about women. Joel Henning wrote of the

Goodman production that:

> Mr. Miller is famously known for sharply delineated characters but
> cardboard women. Critics have often pointed to Linda, Willy's wife,
> as a prime example of a two-dimensional Miller woman. . . .
> Elizabeth Franz, however, transcends Mr. Miller's limitations and
> sustains a measured performance throughout, flawlessly alternating
> between displays of feral strength in defending the declining Willy
> against their sons and a blank submissiveness in the face of Willy's
> bloated ego. Her Linda is pure, clear and relentless.

That Franz should somehow be able to create a Linda that is not to be
found in Miller's dialogue is an interesting notion, but not consistent
with her approach to acting. Franz, who wrote a novel about the
character in preparation for playing the role, delves deeply into a role
as it emerges from the script. She said in an interview: "I understood
the strength a woman needs to survive in a very masculine world. I
grasped Linda's vast, almost superhuman capacity for love, and I
understood that her love for Willy is as overwhelming as it is because
it's deeply sexual." She has described her approach to acting in
terms of Quakerism, which taught her "that we must totally grasp the
cause and nature of others' suffering in order to understand their
motivations and their rages, and we must suspend all judgment of
them." Although she finds some aspects of Linda's character
difficult to accept, she believes that it is part of her craft to find a way
to realize the character on stage as it is written. As a feminist, she
has to work at suspending judgment in order to "play Linda's
unawareness of her oppression" as a "passive enabler whose role is to
boost all of her husband's craziest dreams, and who is therefore
incapable of exposing his delusions and telling him the truth" (Gray
32).

In a similarly intense psychological characterization, Kevin
Anderson has been recognized as an emotionally tortured Biff, rather
than the accusatory truth-teller Biff is sometimes portrayed as. Jack
Helbig said that he "plays Biff as a kind of proto-beatnik, a man so
knotted up with unexpressed anger at his father—and at the rat race
world his father lived for—he cannot bear to be ordered around by
any authority figure." Another critic called Anderson a "terrifying
Biff" because of the intensity of his emotion, but the most common

comment was how much he resembles his father, and how much he is trying not to. Brantley wrote that Anderson "brings extraordinary conviction to the idea of a man struggling not to become his father and losing the battle" (Nov. 3). Falls has chosen to repeat one of the signature gestures of John Malkovich's Biff in having Anderson kiss Willy at the end of the confrontational truth-telling scene that ends act 2. Arthur Miller has said that he became aware in watching this production that *Salesman* is:

> A love story basically between a father and a son. In fact it just occurred to me a couple of weeks ago when I was talking to one of the actors that everyone in this play loves Willy. Everybody, excepting Willy. . . It's about the loss of love and the finding of love again" (*Charlie Rose*).

If, as many critics have suggested, Robert Falls's production of the play de-emphasizes its political and economic implications in order to emphasize its treatment of family relationships, Arthur Miller would seem to approve of this treatment of and for the 1990s. Margaret Spillane has suggested another immediate application to the cultural moment of 1999. The production, she says "is stunning proof that theater, at this moment, may be doing its most radical work in memory":

> Theater reminds people of a literacy that entertainment technologists have made them forget they possess—the ability to read stories directly off the living bodies of other human beings. The retouched, imperishable cinematic action figures morphing through landscapes of immolated skyscrapers and liquidated enemies cannot match the storytelling power of the Loman family's vulnerable skin.

Notes

[1] For good examples of each point of view, see Harold Clurman, "Theatre Attention!" *New Republic* 120 (28 Feb. 1949): 26-28 and Eleanor Clark, "Old Glamour, New Gloom," *Partisan Review* 16 (1949): 631-36.
[2] See, for example, George Ross, "*Death of a Salesman* in the Original,"

Commentary 11 (1951): 184-86; Joel Shatzky, "Arthur Miller's 'Jewish' Salesman," *Studies in American Jewish Literature* 2 (Winter 1976): 1-9; Daniel Walden, "Miller's Roots and His Moral Dilemma: or, Continuity from Brooklyn to *Salesman*" in *Critical Essays on Arthur Miller*, ed. James J. Martine (Boston: G. K. Hall, 1979) 189-96; and Mary McCarthy, "American Realists, Playwrights," *Encounter* 17 (July 1961): 24-31.

Works Cited

Applebome, Peter. "Present at the Birth of a Salesman." *New York Times* 29 Jan. 1999: Weekend B1, 27.

"AOL CHAT with Brian Dennehy." America Online. 21 February 1999.

Brantley, Ben. "A Dark New Production Illuminates 'Salesman.'" *New York Times* 3 Nov. 1998, Tuesday, Late Edition, Final: E1.

---. "Attention Must Be Paid, Again." *New York Times*, 11 Feb. 1999: B1, 5.

Charlie Rose. Television Program. 25 February 1999. Transcript #2365.

Christiansen, Richard. "Golden Revival Proves a Golden Anniversary, for 'Salesman.'" Chicago *Tribune* 29 Sep. 1998.

Feldberg, Robert. "An American Tragedy Rises to the Occasion Again." *The Bergen Record* 11 Feb. 1999.

Gray, Francine Du Plessix. "Leading Ladies." *New Yorker* 15 March 1999: 32-33.

Helbig, Jack. "Rebirth of 'Salesman.'" *Daily Herald* 2 Oct. 1998.

Henning, Joel. "Chicago Theater: 'Salesman' Revived." *Wall Street Journal* 5 Oct. 1998: A28.

Istel, John. "Open House." *Atlantic Monthly* 283.2 (Feb. 1999): 31.

Jones, Chris. "'Death of a Salesman.'" *Variety* 372.8 (5 October 1998): 78.

Karam, Edward. "Child's Play." *Times* (London) 26 Feb. 1999.

Kazan, Elia. "Excerpts from Notebooks for Directing *Death of a Salesman.*" in Kenneth Thorpe Rowe, *A Theater in Your Head*. New York: Funk and Wagnalls, 1960. 44-62.

Klinghoffer, David. "Undying Salesman." *National Review* 51 (8 March 1999): 54.

Lyons, Donald. "Miller's *Death* Gets New Life" *New York Post* 11 Feb. 1999.

Miller, Arthur. *Death of a Salesman*. New York: Viking, 1949.

---. *The Theater Essays of Arthur Miller*. Ed. Robert A. Martin and Steven R. Centola. New York: Da Capo, 1996.

Poling, James. "Handy 'Gadget." *Colliers* 129 (31 May 1952): 56-61.
Rose, Lloyd. "New Life for *A Salesman.*" *Washington Post* 11 Feb. 1999.
Spillane, Margaret. "Life of a Salesman." *The Nation* 268 (8 March 1999):7.
Stearns, David Patrick. "Sterling 'Salesman' and Other Shining Shows in
    Chicago." *USA Today* Final Edition 30 Oct. 1998: Life, E6.
Winer, Linda. "Everyman Revisited." *Newsday* 11 Feb. 1999.

"Attention Must be Paid": Arthur Miller's *Death of a Salesman* and the American Century

Peter Levine

Few plays in the lexicon of the American theatre have had "legs" as long as Arthur Miller's *Death of a Salesman*. Be it on Broadway, stock company, university or community theatre stage, on radio, as feature film or television special, from Berlin to Beijing, it is hard to imagine any play written in the 20th century that has been seen or heard by more people throughout the world or whose language and images have become so much a part of American popular culture.

Over the past few years I have struggled with the possibility of writing a book about this play, one that would take advantage of my own skills as an American social historian and my passion for acting. I even came up with a nice title and a catchy spin. "'Attention Must be Paid': Arthur Miller's *Death of a Salesman* and the American Century" would focus on audience response and on the artists who created its many versions rather than on critics and scholars who have appraised it, in the process, gauging its enduring significance as a window into American culture. Neither a theatre historian nor a literary critic, I would speak instead as a cultural and social historian experienced in exploring the significance of popular culture, particularly for what it tells us about the values and concerns of everyday people. I would also speak as an experienced actor aware of how actors, directors, and others involved in the production process impose themselves between the written text of a play and its audience—how they become, intentionally or not, mediators of culture; of the message and the meaning that a performance produces for a particular audience in a particular time and place.

These impulses drive my desire to understand what the long term popularity of this play tells us about the hopes, fears, and dreams of its audiences and about the culture in which they unfold. How has the meaning of the play endured or changed depending upon time, place, and cultural context? How do different audiences at different moments understand it: the play as opportunity to explore the response of Americans to significant continuities and changes in post World War II America.

The experience has been both wonderful, if at the moment, incomplete. I have had the opportunity to be Ben Loman on stage, rehearse Willy in many scene study classes both in New York and in East Lansing, Michigan, interview Arthur Miller, Douglas Campbell, Jim Houghton of the Signature Theatre Company, which last year devoted its season to Miller, and also talk to a variety of Willys including Dustin Hoffman, Al Waxman, Jim Edmondson, Mel Winkler, and even an occasional Linda. Be it at the New York Public Library for the Performing Arts, the Ransom Center for the Humanities, or the University of Michigan, I have also employed the tools of my trade to exploit archival and manuscript material about Miller and *Salesman*, compiling among other things a fairly complete production history of the play, including everything from major equity stages to local community theatre. These experiences have confirmed my original intent even as they suggest new ways to explore the long term cultural significance of one of Theatre World's most important plays. Let me explain.

My initial approach was to focus on specific moments in the play's production history as a way of exploring what it tells us about ourselves and our culture. The possibilities are certainly rich. For example, consider the following series of events set in motion after the play first opened in New York in February, 1949.

Winner of every major theatre award and the Pulitzer Prize for drama that year, *Death of a Salesman* also became the first play to become a main selection of the Book of the Month Club. Although Arthur Miller chuckled at the news and claims no memory of it ("Quite frankly it has passed through my mind leaving not a trace"), he, along with Herbert Hoover and Ralph Bunche were named one of the ten outstanding fathers of the year by the National Father's Day

Committee, all lauded as American Fathers: Builders of Our Nation's Future (Levine, Interview). Businessmen like A. Howard Fuller, the president of the Fuller Brush Company, praised Miller for recognizing "the professional salesman" as "the cutting edge of a free competitive economy" and "the real hero of American society (Fuller 79). One year after it opened on Broadway, the play embarked on a national tour. And by February, 1950, international productions had already appeared in eleven different countries. Also in the works were plans by Columbia Pictures to turn the play into a feature film directed by Stanley Kramer.

By the time the film was ready for release in 1951, however, the United States was in the grip of growing anti-Communist hysteria. Columbia Pictures shot a trailer for the film in which business school professors, as Arthur Miller remembers, "blithely explained that Willy Loman was entirely atypical...[and that] nowadays, selling was a fine profession with limitless spiritual compensations" (Miller, *Timebends* 315). Although his threatened lawsuit successfully kept the trailer from being shown, he was not able to prevent pickets at performances of the play both in the United States and in Europe protesting his alleged communist sympathies. Five years later, Miller would be called to testify before the House un-American Activities Committee.

In November, 1954, *Death of a Salesman* made news again. Three weeks before the opening of its three night run, the Glen Players of Glenwood Landing, on Long Island's North Shore, learned that Thomas Paradine, a national vice commander of the American Legion, charter member of the community theatre company, a Coca Cola executive and its "Willy," had decided to withdraw from the role. According to the *New York Post*, Paradine backed out after conducting "a personal investigation of Miller's background, triggered by concerns from his American Legion Post that the playwright was associated with "left-wing groups." John Foley, commander of the post, was even more direct in explaining why he chose not to attend the play. "After all," he noted, "the play was written by a man who was brought up before the House Un-American Activities Committee, even though he hadn't been proven guilty" (*Post*).

Fortunately for director Sally Bullock and the Glen Cove players, a replacement was found. The show played to sold-out houses at the Glenwood Landing school auditorium. "Tommy was just right for the part," Bullock noted. "He was big and mature looking. . .He has a right to his own opinions," she concluded, but fortunately none of the other players agreed with him." In the end, according to the *New York Times*, the players agreed that *Death of a Salesman* was "excellent theatre" that contains nothing "un-American or offensive to anyone."

In the short space of five years and often at the same time, different audiences "read" *Death of a Salesman* quite differently: from unvarnished, patriotic celebration of the American Way to criticism of it, all during a time when a Cold War Communist witch hunt often painted alleged subversives as effeminate, weak, homosexuals—not real American men.

The connections are not unimportant. Untangling the cultural meanings of such events suggests that its popularity across American time and place has much to do with the way in which it resonates with audiences bred on certain longstanding social constructions of American masculinity and capitalism.

Let me be clear here. As actor, historian, and a second-generation Brooklyn Jewish man who comes from the same territory, both literally and figuratively as Willy, Linda, Happy and Biff, I know that at its heart the play is about love and loss, about family, about dreams denied and unfulfilled, about fathers and sons in search of each other. Clearly such concerns help account for its international appeal. As Miller told me, "I've never written about issues. I've written about what happens to people under certain circumstances. The issues have always been the occasion of the play, not the theme of the play." In the American context, however. Whatever else *Death of a Salesman* is about, it is most significantly about the lure of American capitalism intertwined with a cult of masculinity socially cut from the bowels of the American past.

Take, for example, Ben Loman, the personification of the archetypal American capitalist—the swashbuckling, arrogant, individual whose masculinity is defined by strength, power, aggression, competitiveness, toughness and a win at all costs mentality. As an actor portraying Ben, I hoped I made the audience feel the demonic power I feel on stage when I turn to Willy in the last scene and say "The boat, we'll be late," ensnaring him with the force of my physical presence (itself a fantasy of Willy's tortured soul) and the glint in my eye as I take him to his suicide in the service of Mammon and Masculinity—the twin engines of the American Century and Willy's doomsday machine.

Carving his success and fortune in African and Alaskan frontiers,

Ben seems a curious throwback to frontier America, out of place as a hero in the corporate, white collar world of the 1950s. Yet this dominant brand of American masculinity has been with us since the days of Daniel Boone and Andrew Jackson. It encompasses a long line of physical champions that span the worlds of John L. Sullivan, Babe Ruth, and O.J. Simpson. Is it any wonder that as late as 1995, according to a Harris Poll, America's favorite movie star was John Wayne, dead already for fourteen years! (Wills 11)

There are costs involved here. For too long women were denied the legitimacy of feelings and possibilities defined as masculine; forced either to mask them in order to make it in a man's world or subject to ridicule and marginalization if they chose to openly express them.

American men, too, have paid a price. The power of this dominant version of masculinity makes it very difficult for many men to accept their own feelings of vulnerability and weakness that are normative for any human being or to feel empathetic towards those who do not fit the mold. And as George Chauncey has shown us in *Gay New York: Gender, Urban Culture and the Making of the Gay Male World, 1890-1940*, in particular cultural contexts, this failure can lead to outright hostility and violence towards homosexuals whose behavior, attitude, and sexual preference do not meet conventional expectations.

As I have written elsewhere, the power and popularity of such images, be it Ben Loman, or American male athletes cut from the same mold—Arnold Palmer, Vince Lombardi, and Mickey Mantle come immediately to mind—were never stronger than in Cold War America (Lipsyte). Their popularity accompanied a resurgent distinction of gender that demanded a sharp separation of male and female roles, reminding Americans of a time when "men were men" and women were all but excluded from public life. Although gender relations have certainly changed in the last half-century, this social construction of masculinity still remains a powerful force in our culture.

Willy's embrace of this version of masculinity, I suspect is both his problem and ultimately part of his appeal. Like many white American males then and now, Willy aspires to such models. The culture and times in which he lives demand it, as Miller so perceptively understands. But such concerns are not removed from the basic matters of love and loss, of fathers and sons, that dominate this play. The very theme of love between fathers and sons, as Willy understands it, is inextricably linked to this connection between capitalism and masculinity.

Willy cannot imagine being loved unless he is "successful" within this particular definition of American masculinity. He cannot imagine being accepted, appreciated or admired by his sons unless he has succeeded in a competitive, conquering, individualistic way. He cannot imagine that he can be loved as he is—a needy, vulnerable but well-intentioned man out of place with his times. Even when he finally recognizes that Biff loves him, he misses the boat. Accept us for who we are, not for our phony dreams, Biff pleads, even as Willy denies the possibility by offering him the only gift that makes sense to him within his construction of masculinity—a $20,000 gift, the price of his own life—to launch Biff's success. "That boy. . .that boy is going to be. . .magnificent," he tells Ben at the end of the play; no different from the sentiments he expresses to Linda in its opening scene when he proposes getting Biff a job selling. "He could be big in no time," he tells her.

I tried this out on Arthur Miller when we met last February. He didn't disagree but suggested that I was "looking at it from the American viewpoint." The play, he reminded me, "has the same effect" on people throughout the world wherever it has been staged. Leaning back in his chair (Did he make it himself, I wondered, with those immense hands that engulfed mine in a warm handshake when we first met and that made me think immediately of Willy Loman, never so happy than with a batch of cement.), he mused for a moment and added: "I have to come back to the fact that it's just a damn good play. That's why it works, you see!"

Not only for Miller and millions of people worldwide who have seen or read *Death of a Salesman* and have taken from it their own meanings, but also for those who bend it to their own political and commercial purposes and who have made the play's language part of the American vernacular, even if, at times, seemingly at odds with Miller's own politics and sensibilities. "Oh yeah, I know that," Miller laughed, amused by the news that the Republican National Committee had included excerpts from the play in a book it had compiled called, *A Call to Character*. "It penetrates society, which is what you want. . .People are going to make completely different things out of it. And if the work itself has a certain human vitality, that will happen more than less. If it doesn't have that kind of vitality, it's not likely to happen."

This conference alone is testament to *Salesman*'s vitality. The many interviews I have conducted and the comments of playwrights and writers in the most recent issue of the *Michigan Quarterly Review*, devoted to Arthur Miller, confirm it: the play's ability to inspire people to their own art even as it allows them to grapple with their own American stories. And that, finally, is how my own work is now taking shape: a book about the play through the stories of artists and everyday people affected by it, told in ways that hopefully address underlying themes about American culture and values in the 20th century.

In that spirit, let me offer you one such story, expressed in verse, that suggests the power of the play and even its redemptive possibilities, if not for Willy, then at least for the poet. It comes from a young New York playwright who sent it to Miller after watching a version of *Death of a Salesman* on television in 1973. In part, it read:

> Dear Arthur Miller
> I just want you to know what you did to me tonight.
> I just finished watching your play on television.
> I'm exhausted.
> I'm feeling so many things. . .
> Most of all you showed me
> My father.
> The sunshine junkie.
> The man who thinks the world judges him by the smile
> on his face.
> Who puts the virtue of being
> liked above everything.
> Who measures and respects another
> Man because of a silver cigarette case.
> But you also showed me
> the man who only wants to be loved by his son.
> And that I don't need a reason to love him (Miller Collection).

Notes

Fuller, A. Howard. "A Salesman is Everybody." *Fortune Magazine*, May, 1949, 79+.

Levine, Peter. Arthur Miller, February 25, 1998. Other references that refer to conversation with Miller took place on this date.

Lipsyte, Robert and Peter Levine. *Idols of the Game: A Sporting History of the American Century*. Atlanta: 1995. See also, Levine, Peter. *Ellis Island to Ebbets Field: Sport and the American Jewish Experience*. New York: 1992.

Miller, Arthur. Fan Mail File, August 8, 1973. Arthur Miller Collection,

Harry Ransom Center for the Humanities, University of Texas.
---. *Timebends, A Life.* New York, 1987.
New York Post. December 10, 1954.
New York Times. November 12 and December 10, 1954.
Wills, Garry. *John Wayne's America.* New York, 1997.

"The Condition of Tension": Unity of Opposites as Dramatic Form and Vision in Arthur Miller's *Death of a Salesman*

Steven R. Centola

Few American plays have achieved the notoriety of *Death of a Salesman*. Winner of both the Pulitzer Prize and the New York Drama Critics' Circle Award in 1949, *Death of a Salesman* has attained worldwide recognition as one of the best plays ever to emerge from the American theater. In fact, not only is this celebrated play generally viewed as one of only a handful of truly great American plays; it is also regarded by many as a classic of the modern stage. This riveting drama about the Loman family's desperate struggle for love and understanding has been produced in virtually every major city in the world and has been translated into at least twenty-nine different languages. As Richard Shickel observes, "It has been claimed that not a night passes without *Salesman* being performed somewhere in the world, usually with success, mostly in venues where no one can possibly conceive of what America was like in 1949" (330). No better evidence of the play's universal appeal exists than in the audience's passionate response to *Salesman* in Beijing in 1983, where the Chinese people, according to Miller, discovered "the Lomans in themselves" (*Salesman in Beijing* 249). This quintessentially American play staked common ground between two radically opposed cultures and validated Miller's belief that, beneath the surface differences determined by race, geography, or ideology, there exists "only one humanity" (*Salesman in Beijing* 5). Its successful production in China and in venues all over the world leaves no doubt that Miller's play transcends national boundary lines and transmutes a typically American situation involving the pursuit of the golden dream of success into a universally significant vision of the eternal conflict between parents and children, men and women, and self and society.

Whether it is viewed as a tragedy of the common man, a social drama indicting capitalism and American business ethics, a sociological consideration of work alienation and its impact on identity, a cultural critique of the American family and stereotypical gender roles in American society, a modern morality play about today's Everyman, or a complex psychological study of guilt, repression, and psychosis, *Death of a Salesman* is a compelling drama that makes for an intensely moving and hauntingly memorable theatrical experience. Whether it is produced in America or abroad, *Death of a Salesman* never fails to send shock waves across its audiences with what Robert Coleman once called its "emotional dynamite" (360). The power of this play has long been celebrated by the critics. Following its opening night performance at the Morosco Theater in 1949, Howard Barnes fervently praised the play's "majesty, sweep and shattering dramatic impact" (358). Likewise, in one of *Salesman*'s earliest reviews, Ward Morehouse, also struck by the play's "intensity," concludes that Miller's "poignant, shattering and devastating drama" is "numbing in sheer power" (360). During its run on Broadway in 1975, Douglas Watt wrote: "This early Miller triumph continues to provide a shattering emotional experience. . ." (221). And, in 1984, as Dustin Hoffman imbued the salesman with warmth and charm in his spectacular performance at the Broadhurst Theater, Watt again noted "that the power and compassion of Miller's masterpiece are still capable of moving us deeply. . ." (328). Similar reviews accompanied the Chinese production in 1983 and the television version in 1985, which is estimated to have reached an audience of about twenty-five million people. Tom Shales sums up the critical response to the television version best as he writes: "Tremendous and thrilling and eloquently sorrowful, the new CBS production of Arthur Miller's play . . . is going to stand as a monument in modern television. . ." (C1, C7). Fifty years after its original production, the play continues to receive favorable reviews, as is evident from Ben Brantley's commentary on the current production of *Salesman* at the O'Neill Theater. Moved by Brian Dennehy's "majestic" and "heartbreaking" performance and Robert Falls's "powerhouse staging" (B1), Brantley praises "the almost operatic emotional sweep" (B5) of the latest "harrowing revival" (B1) of Arthur Miller's masterpiece.

Over the years, there certainly has been no shortage of superlatives in the critical response to *Death of a Salesman*, and for good reason. Miller succeeds in accomplishing here what many others have failed to do. What mainly distinguishes *Death of a Salesman* from other American plays of this century, writes Esther Merle Jackson, is that "Much of the text of *Death of a Salesman* is given to the articulation of the sensuous form of the poetic image" (72). Like Eugene O'Neill and Tennessee Williams, Miller, says Jackson, creates poetry in the theater by employing "as the instrumentation of vision, a complex theatre symbol: a union of gesture, word, and music; light, color, and pattern; rhythm and movement" (73). This remarkable fusion gives the play its rich texture and allows the playwright to succeed in his effort to capture "the veritable countenance of life" (*Introduction* to *Collected Plays* 30). To achieve this effect, Miller deliberately set out to make the form of the play reflect the process of Willy's mind, a feat realized through Miller's skillful use of what he calls his "cinematographic" structure (*Introduction* to *Collected Plays* 26). The form of the play is designed to reveal "a mobile concurrency of past and present" (*Introduction* to *Collected Plays* 26) in Willy's mind and his inner conflict as the two collide, shattering his illusions and forcing him into direct confrontation with the unforeseen consequences of his past choices. The "friction, collision, and tension between past and present," notes Miller, "was the heart of the play's particular construction" (*Introduction* to *Collected Plays* 27). The degree to which this construction works and results in the unity of form, character, and action largely accounts for much of the play's success.

In writing about his search for the appropriate form for this play, Miller explains why he decided it was necessary to incorporate paradox into his dramatic strategy. Miller says:

> I sought the relatedness of all things by isolating their unrelatedness, a man superbly alone with his sense of not having touched and finally

knowing in his last extremity that the love which had always been in the room unlocated was now found. The image of a suicide so mixed in motive as to be unfathomable and yet demanding statement . . .the image of private man in a world full of strangers. It came from structural images. The play's eye was to revolve from within Willy's head, sweeping endlessly in all directions like a light on the sea. . . . It was thought of as having the density of the novel form in its interchange of viewpoints, so that while all roads led to Willy the other characters were to feel it was their play, a story about them and not him. There were two undulating lines in mind, one above the other, the past webbed to the present moving on together in him and sometimes openly joined and once, finally, colliding. Above all in the structural sense, I aimed to make a play with the veritable countenance of life. To make one the many, as in life, so that "society" is a great power and a mystery of custom and inside the man and surrounding him, as the fish is in the sea and the sea inside the fish, his birthplace and burial ground, promise and threat. The image of a play without transitional scenes was there in the beginning . . .to make the form give and stretch and contract for the sake of the thing to be said. To cling to the process of Willy's mind as the form the story would take (*Introduction* to *Collected Plays* 30-31).

Miller's comments reveal his conscious decision to unite oppositional forces in his play and use the play's form, which mirrors and embodies Willy's internal conflict, as the primary means of showing the underlying tension that results from the reciprocal pull of dialectical forces in his principal character's life. Willy's situation, though, while extraordinary in many respects, may ultimately be more representative than we might like to admit. Most people at some time in their lives feel the powerful force of society operating within them as they struggle against its pressure to conform and attempt to maintain their individuality. Likewise, at some point we all sense the surge of time endlessly flowing in our minds as memories mingle with conscious thought patterns or take surrealistic shape in dreams. Past and present certainly live within all of us. The contradictory impulses that wage a war inside Willy Loman are the bane of human existence. *Salesman*'s success, therefore, lies in Miller's ability to find a form that not only reveals the inner workings of Willy Loman's disoriented mind, but that also comments on the paradoxical condition that defines human existence: the constant struggle within the individual between self and society, right and wrong, love and hate, consciousness and unconsciousness, success and failure, joy and sorrow, work and play, past and present, life and death. Life is flux and, and as Miller, O'Neill, and other great writers have repeatedly demonstrated, human life is frequently characterized by internal conflict. If the value of a human life may ultimately be determined by the extent to which an individual struggles against contradictory impulses in an effort to give existence purpose and meaning, then it is easy to see why *Death of a Salesman* is so popular and successful and still continues to move audiences all around the world. Willy's battle is ours too, for despite his particular failings and idiosyncrasies, Willy Loman's futile effort to resist reduction and atomization and his constant flight from his alienated condition reflect a universal need for personal triumph over the forces that deny individuality and constantly threaten to diminish our humanity.

This condition of tension that Miller captures in the form of *Death of a Salesman* is evident in virtually every aspect of the play. It is inherent in the complex interrelationship between opposed loyalties and ideals in Willy's mind that motivate every facet of his speech and behavior. It is evident as well in the dramatic interplay between Willy and other characters in the play, not only those present—like Biff, Happy, and Linda Loman, but also significant figures mentioned by Willy who have helped to shape his values or have played some role in the formation of his personality and sense of self-esteem— such as his father, his brother, Ben, and his greatest inspiration: Dave Singleman. The condition of tension can also be seen in the play's unusual style—Miller's remarkable fusion of realism and expressionism—as well as in the unity of text and subtext, image and word, gesture and sound, music and lighting, reality and illusion, and character and action in the play. Miller combines expressionism—in the lighting, music, distorted time sequence, and surrealistic scenes with Ben—with the psychological realism most vividly found in Willy's characterization through such aspects of his behavior as his gestures, intonation, speech rhythms, facial expressions, and body language. Through his careful integration of the realistic and surrealistic aspects of the play, Miller not only allows his audience to see the inner workings and strange logic of Willy's mind, but he does so in such a way that ensures that everything Willy says and does retains a strong sense of probability. In this way, what is essentially impossible to view in a realistic manner—the stream of consciousness inside a person's head—is presented to the audience in viable dramatic terms.

This dialectical tension is also present in other ways. As the action unfolds and Willy plods unyieldingly toward the suicide that he views as his personal triumph, the spellbound audience cannot help but anticipate the eventual outcome while simultaneously wishing that what must come to pass will never occur. The audience feels the force of necessity that governs Willy's actions even while observing the salesman's irrational resistance to the factors that control his destiny. This clash between the actual and the imagined works on us subliminally and affects our response to Willy's dilemma. We come to understand and perhaps even share his desperate conviction that he must at once both pursue and yet hide from the truth. Everything presented in the play contributes in some way to the audience's awareness of the condition of tension that defines *Salesman*'s form and vision.

Perhaps the most obvious and important way the condition of tension is revealed is through the characterization of Willy Loman. Wanting to establish and manifest this strong correlation between form and vision as he sketched out his ideas for this play, Miller initially entitled it *The Inside of His Head* and planned to design the set in the shape of a person's skull. Miller tells us: "The first image that occurred to me which was to result in *Death of a Salesman* was of an enormous face the height of the proscenium arch which would appear and then open up, and we would see the inside of a man's head" (*Introduction* to *Collected Plays* 23). Even without such a conspicuous title or set design, *Death of a Salesman* clearly relies on the strength of Willy's characterization for the expression of the playwright's artistic vision. Willy literally dominates the play. It is designed to give outward expression to his inner fears, desires, and contradictions. As the lights brighten and the music signals Willy's nostalgic reenactments of the past, Willy appears spry, amusing, and cheerful. But as his attention shifts back to present concerns or sorrows, his behavior suddenly becomes quarrelsome, insulting, and sullen. Oftentimes this rapid transformation occurs as the lights darken and the music ends. This blend of stage devices gives outward form to Willy's "*mercurial nature*" (*Salesman* 131) and makes us sharply aware of the subterranean tensions dividing Willy.

The complexity of the tension that makes Willy Loman both a splintered personality and an interesting person is also evident in the disparity between the hollowness of his words and the sincere passion with which he expresses them. His frequent and spontaneous utterance of platitudes and success formulas reveal not only the poverty of his language, but also his deep feeling about and inadequate understanding of fatherhood, salesmanship, and success in one's personal life as well as in the business world in American society. For Willy, "personality always wins the day" (*Salesman* 151), but the play offers a contrasting perspective in the examples of successful businessmen like Charley, Howard Wagner, and Willy's dead brother, Ben, and in the reference to J. P. Morgan—figures who prove that one can become financially successful without exactly having a winning personality. Willy's reliance on clichés also reveals that he does not recognize how his bromidic language is actually used to bolster his own faltering self-confidence. Willy turns the success-formula platitudes into his personal mantra. By passionately repeating hackneyed phrases, he subconsciously attempts to assure himself that he has made the right choices in his life, but what he fails to recognize is that this very insistence has only served to prevent him from questioning and understanding his past choices and conduct and their effects on his relations with others.

Ironically, therefore, Willy's speech shows that he both embraces and rejects the life-lie that has destroyed his family. Even though he has lived his entire life striving to attain material success, Willy has clearly wanted more than material prosperity out of life. For at least the last sixteen years of his life, more than anything else, Willy has consciously sought to regain his family's love and respect, and through attaining that, he subconsciously hoped to restore his own lost dignity and diminished self-esteem. The guilt that has tormented him since his infidelity was discovered by Biff in the hotel room in Boston only serves to aggravate his already disturbed condition. Divided between the demands of the family and the pressures of his career, which must have been enormous since he had to work and support his family during the days of the Great Depression, Willy unwittingly accelerates his own skid toward self-destruction by clinging fiercely to cultural myths and stereotypes that only serve to quicken his withdrawal from reality.

Miller displays the gravity of Willy's glide into his private world of dreams and illusions through his use of the surrealistic scenes in which Willy reenacts the past. In these memory scenes, Miller suggests that Willy's inner division has much to do with his confusion over his identity and his uncertainty about value formation. Abandoned at an early age by his father, Willy has tried all of his life to compensate for this painful loss. This early experience of betrayal and abandonment is compounded by the equally disturbing disappearance of his older brother. With the two men from his childhood family virtually abandoning him as they venture off in search of their own personal dreams, Willy finds himself alienated from the community of men and nearly completely loses his sense of his own identity as a male. His insecurity about his identity is evident in the memory scene where he confesses to Ben that he feels "kind of temporary" (*Salesman* 159) about himself and seeks his brother's assurance that he is doing a good job of bringing up his sons. "I'm afraid that I'm not teaching them the right kind of—Ben, how should I teach them?" asks Willy (*Salesman* 159). However, even though Willy seems to idolize Ben and treasure his advice and opinions, Willy rarely does what Ben suggests. In fact, until the end of act 2, when Ben appears entirely as a figment of Willy's troubled imagination in a scene that has little to do with any remembered episode from the past, Willy implicitly rejects Ben's lifestyle and approach to business. Ben, therefore, embodies more than just the image of success in Willy's mind; in many ways, he can be viewed as Willy's alter ego. Ben is the other self that Willy might have become had he decided to live by a different code of ethics. For, unlike Ben, who abandoned the family and screwed on his fists to fight for his fortune in Alaska and Africa, Willy stayed in Brooklyn with his family—perhaps even cared for his mother before her death—and embraced a different approach to business than that which is exemplified by his brother. Willy turned to a model from the past and patterned his life on Dave Singleman's example: the legendary eighty-four year-old salesman who sold merchandise in thirty-one states by picking up his telephone in his hotel room and calling buyers who loved him. Just as Ben is the embodiment of one kind of American dream to Willy, so too is Dave Singleman representative of another kind—and that dichotomy is also part of Willy's confusion: both men symbolize the American dream, yet in Willy's mind they represent value systems that are diametrically opposed to each other. The memory scenes, therefore, are important in bringing out this contrast and in showing what Willy's thoughts about Ben reflect about his own conflicting values.

Miller further uses the memory scenes to display the condition of tension by showing how the weight of Ben's authority in Willy's mind is counterbalanced by the equally powerful influence of other characters. This counterbalancing effect seems designed to show that, while Ben has had a significant impact on Willy's past that continues to remain alive in the present in his imagination, Ben's influence on Willy over the years has actually been no greater than that which has been exerted upon him by such characters as Linda and Dave Singleman, who perhaps had the most profound impact on Willy since he exists in Willy's mind exclusively as an idealized image.

Throughout *Death of a Salesman*, Miller externalizes warring factions within Willy's fractured psyche through the dynamic and oftentimes contentious interaction of the play's characters. Each character essentially expresses a different part of Willy's personality. Linda stirs his guilt and pricks his conscience with her loyalty, devotion, and affection; Charley's common sense and practicality pull Willy toward an honest confrontation with his situation; Ben's pride and arrogance reflect Willy's own egotistical drive for self-assertion and self-fulfillment; Biff gives voice to Willy's own poetic struggle for meaning and purpose in life; Happy, on the other hand, merely verbalizes Willy's lies, dreams, and self-delusion. These forces fiercely compete against each other, struggling for dominance over Willy, but although one might temporarily rise in prominence over the others, no one maintains control indefinitely. All remain active within Willy, leaving him divided, disturbed, and confused.

And, significantly, Willy is not the only character in *Salesman* who experiences this condition. In his stage directions, Miller describes both Biff and Happy as "*lost*" and "*confused*" (*Salesman* 136). They have inherited different parts of Willy's personality and have acquired both his powerful dreams and their society's myths, but they also lack any genuine understanding of how best to attain their own American dream. Happy completely succumbs to the lure of the cultural myth of success, but after wrestling with his conscience and deciding not to conform to his father's expectations and live his lies, Biff momentarily shatters the Loman life-lie in an effort to free himself and save his father's life. Ironically, this very act of love serves as the catalyst for Willy's death. After suffering years of guilty torment and self-punishment, Willy gets concrete proof of his son's love. Rather than risk losing the precious but tenuous connection that now binds him to Biff, Willy decides to end his life and guarantee that he will no longer incur the wrath, condemnation, and scorn of those he truly loves. The Requiem scene, however, implies that his suicide may have had the opposite effect of what it was designed to achieve.

Standing over his father's grave, Biff rejects Willy's life and says: "He had all the wrong dreams. All, all, wrong. . . He never knew who he was" (*Salesman* 221). The play shows that Biff is at least partially right. Willy does deny the value of his aptitude for manual labor, and he lives his life pursuing false dreams and running away from his responsibility for his failures and failings. However, Biff only sees part of the picture. Charley is also right in saying: "A salesman is got to dream, boy. It comes with the territory" (*Salesman* 222). While Charley may literally be referring to the necessity to embrace the dream of success in American society as a cultural inheritance that drives the capitalist establishment, Miller deliberately plants this important speech at the play's end to emphasize the inescapable conditions of human existence that compel us all to dream. The territory Charley alludes to really belongs to all of us. It is the psychic map of humanity that makes us long for an unalienated existence and a life that is not devoid of purpose and meaning. Miller's vivid use of a metaphorical contrast best describes our alienated condition. He says: "We wish so for a pillow to lay our head upon, and it's a stone" (*Conversation* 29). Life *is* change, conflict, tension, a war of wills and desires, an everlasting struggle to bring order to chaos and impose meaning on a fundamentally absurd world. It is the entropic condition that Willy resists, and because of Willy's fierce determination to fight his impossible battle against the inherent conditions of life and human existence, Miller writes: "There is a nobility . . . in Willy's struggle. Maybe it comes from his refusal to relent, to give up" *(Beijing* 27). Against all odds, Willy demands that life have "meaning and significance and honor" (*Beijing* 49). Willy, says Miller, "is trying to lift up a belief in immense redeeming human possibilities" (*Beijing* 29). This is the attraction and glory of Willy Loman, and this limitless hope in the face of hopelessness is also what ultimately defines the tragic spirit of Miller's vision in *Death of a Salesman.*

Miller's play gives us an unblinking look at the terrifying darkness that lies coiled within existence, but attendant to this dark vision is also the discovery that the light enkindled by human kindness and love can give human life a brilliance and luster that will never be extinguished. Willy dies, but death does not defeat Willy Loman; as the Requiem demonstrates, his memory will continue to live on in others. Through his remarkable fusion of opposites that express both the form and the vision of the play, Miller reveals the condition of tension that is life and human existence. Because of its perfect integration of form, character, and action, *Death of a Salesman* is unquestionably a modern masterpiece—one that, as Chris Bigbsy so eloquently states, "celebrates . . .the miracle of human life, in all its bewilderments, its betrayals, its denials, but, finally, and most significantly, its transcendent worth" (*Poet* 723).

Works Cited

Barnes, Howard. "A Great Play Is Born." *New York Theatre Critics' Reviews.* Ed. Rachel W. Coffin 10 (1949): 360.

Bigsby, Christopher. "Arthur Miller: Poet." *Michigan Quarterly Review* 37 (Fall 1998): 713-724.

Brantley, Ben. "Attention Must Be Paid, Again." *New York Times* 11 February 1999: B1, B5.

Centola, Steve. *Arthur Miller in Conversation.* Dallas: Northouse & Northouse, 1993.

Coleman, Robert. "'*Death of a Salesman*' Is Emotional Dynamite." *New York Theatre Critics' Reviews.* Ed. Rachel W. Coffin 10 (1949): 360.

Jackson, Esther Merle. "*Death of a Salesman*: Tragic Myth in the Modern Theatre." *College Language Association Journal* 7 (September 1963): 63-76.

Miller, Arthur. *Death of a Salesman. Arthur Miller's Collected Plays.* Vol. 1. New York: Viking, 1957. 129-222.

---. Introduction. *Arthur Miller's Collected Plays.* Vol. 1. New York: Viking, 1957. 3-55.

---. *Salesman in Beijing.* New York: Viking, 1984.

Morehouse, Ward. "Triumph at the Morosco." *New York Theatre Critics' Reviews.* Ed. Rachel W. Coffin 10 (1949): 360.

Shales, Tom. "Spellbinding '*Salesman*' on CBS." *The Washington Post* 14 September 1985: C1, C7.

Shickel, Richard. "Rebirth of an American Dream." *New York Theatre Critics' Reviews.* Eds. Joan Marlowe and Betty Blake 45 (1984): 330.

Watt, Douglas. "Scott in Miller's '*Salesman*.'" New York Theatre Critics' Reviews. Eds. Joan Marlowe and Betty Blake 36 (1975): 221.

---. "*Death of a Salesman*: Hoffman Shines in Glorious Rebirth of Miller's Drama." *New York Theater Critics' Reviews.* Eds. Joan Marlowe and Betty Blake 45 (1984): 328.

Masculine and Feminine
in *Death of a Salesman*

Heather Cook Callow

No one disputes the importance of Arthur Miller's *Death of a Salesman* in the American drama canon. It is, as Gayle Austin has observed, "the Oedipus Rex of American drama for many people" (63). As such it has occasioned a good deal of critical wrangling, particularly over the nature and stature of its protagonist Willy Loman. Several critics, Harold Bloom among them, consider Miller himself to be confused as to his intentions or at least their execution (*Loman* 1-2; Driver 22-23), and certainly the play's conclusion may be read as unclear regarding what specific values it condemns or advocates. In the Requiem, Biff condemns Willy's dreams as "all wrong" while Charlie, elsewhere a realistic and trustworthy friend to Willy, excuses him, saying a salesman has to dream. I suggest that part of the confusion stems from the melange of typically "masculine" and "feminine" interactional traits, values, and achievements that Miller gives to his characters. In his opening stage directions, Miller describes the imaginary wall lines of Willy's house, pointing out that their boundaries will be broken by the characters as they move into the past. Even so, I suggest, set boundaries between "masculine" and "feminine," as traditionally construed, have also been broken within the play. An examination of these broken boundaries in light of Deborah Tannen's, *You Just Don't Understand: Men and Women in Conversation*, a study of gender associated linguistic patterns and the values they reflect, leads me to suggest that readers have found Willy Loman lacking, in part, because the values he espouses are, strangely enough, primarily "feminine," those that Tannen finds women bring to interaction and to the workplace.

To set the stage, I need first to catalog briefly specific criticisms raised against Willy Loman that correlate with Tannen's gender paradigm.   The first series focuses upon Willy's concept of the necessary criteria for success. Henry Popkin observes that "Willy . . . believes, with Dale Carnegie, that success is the reward of making friends and influencing people" (*Loman* 12). Ivor Brown reports that in England Willy was taken as "a poor, flashy, self-deceiving little man," whose obsession with popularity was more contemptible than natural (*Loman* 5). Arthur Ganz says, "Willy is a man so foolish as to believe that success in the business world can be achieved not by work and ability but by being 'well-liked,' by a kind of hearty popularity that will open all doors and provide favors and preferential treatment" (*Loman* 22).   Robert N. Wilson labels these beliefs "Willy's warped dicta for success" (80). In a more psychological vein, Wilson observes, "Willy attempts to be the person he thinks others desire" (81), and Raymond Williams similarly declares, "Loman is a man who from selling things has passed to selling himself and has become in effect a commodity" (*Loman* 15).

The last few quotations emphasize what Miller himself identified as a playwright's central problem—bridging "the deep split between the private life of man and his social life" (Overland 53). Commenting on Willy's attempt to secure an office job from his boss, Paul Blumberg remarks, his "appeal—so strange and incongruous for a hard headed salesman—is an appeal to 'family relations'" (58). Stephen Lawrence, observing a similar breakdown of the boundary between private and public life says:

> Perhaps what is wrong with society is not that it has implanted the wrong values in him, values which finally do not lead to success anyway, but that it has lost touch with values which should never be relegated only to the personal sphere or the family unit. . . .Willy's problem is that he is human enough to think that the same things that matter in the family—especially his love for his son—matter everywhere, including the world of social success (57).

Finally, and perhaps reflecting upon all of these "shortcomings," John Beaufort insists that Willy is not tragic but sad and that he "will not for one minute accept Willy Loman as the American 'Everyman'" (*Loman* 45).

"Warped," "unnatural," "foolish," "incongruous," inadequate as an American "Everyman"—these are the terms used to characterize Willy's values, his desire to be the person others wish him to be, his wrongheaded confusion of the private and the public, with Lawrence's caveat that perhaps society could benefit from a more personal approach to public intercourse. What may seem warped, unnatural and incongruous coming from a male speaker may, however, as Tannen's study reveals, be quite acceptable coming from a female speaker.

The sociolinguistic approach that Tannen employs shows, through a series of recorded and reported conversations and examples, that American girls and boys grow up in different cultures and that talk between American men and women is consequently cross cultural communication, with each group's patterns of speech showing distinguishable characteristics. Her study provides several observations that are pertinent to *Death of a Salesman* which, one must remember, is subtitled *Certain Private Conversations in Two Acts and a Requiem.* Tannen finds that men view the world hierarchically and that to them in any interaction, conversational or behavioral, one is either one up or one down from the others involved (24-25). This certainly fits Willy and his boys. It is this sentiment that prevents Willy from accepting a job from Charlie and that feeds Happy's notion that "to come out number one man" is "the only dream you can have" (139). Linda, in contrast, asks, "Why must everyone conquer the world?" (85) Willy also appears to fit the masculine model that Tannen finds in his practice of boasting of his personal accomplishments (Tannen 219). In several other respects, however, his talk and his behavior better fit the feminine model. Tannen asserts that women approach the world as a network of connections and that when they pursue status, it is in the guise of connection. She states, "Girls and women feel it is crucial that they be liked by their peers. . . .Boys and men feel it is crucial that they be respected by their peers. . ." (108).

The number of lines Willy speaks that testify to the importance to him of personal connections and being "well-liked" are legion. He asserts, "personality always wins the day" (65) and tries to bring that to bear in his conversation with his boss Howard. His appeal is to personal relations—his relationship with Howard's father, that he remembers the day Howard was born and named—but Howard's approach is hierarchical. He calls Willy "kid" and says "where am I going to put you . . . ?" (80) To his older brother Ben, who achieved his own financial success mining for diamonds and is suspicious of intangible assets, he asserts, "It's not what you do . . .It's who you know and the smile on your face! It's contacts, Ben, contacts!" (86) Even when he speaks of his professional hero, Dave Singleman, he speaks not of Singleman's wealth, but of his being "remembered and loved and helped by so many different people" (81). Singleman's clients were not purchasing a product, they were helping and loving Dave Singleman. In like manner, Willy envisions his own funeral as a testimony to Biff of his personal popularity. These qualities—helping and being helped, being connected and remembered, experiencing and demonstrating solidarity—are all qualities Tannen finds valued more by women than by men.

Willy tells Ben, "That's the wonder. . .of this country that a man can end with diamonds here on the basis of being liked" (86). Granted Willy is speaking in the context of diamond mines, but if one substitutes the word *woman* for *man* here, the statement is not only perfectly understandable but actually truer. Diamonds are a glamorous choice as a commodity, but the association with women's engagement and anniversary jewelry, the feminine jewelry of personal connection and promise is inescapable. Willy's belief that personal attractiveness and personality are his most important assets is much more a traditionally socialized "feminine" attitude than a "masculine" one. Willy comments frequently on Biff's "personal attractiveness," and, when he learns that Biff has gone to see Bill Oliver about a business deal, asks, "How did he dress?" (72), traditionally a quintessentially "feminine" question. When he ponders his own disappointments in the business world he likewise speculates, "I'm not dressing to advantage, maybe" (37). The parlaying of external attractiveness and charm into economic success has historically been a socially acceptable and indeed inculcated "feminine" objective, but one readers are unaccustomed to hearing from a male speaker. Indeed Charlie, at one point, exclaims in exasperation to Willy, "Why must everyone like you? Who liked J.P. Morgan?" (97). Charlie's focus, like that of the men in Tannen's study, is upon respect not popularity.

The commodification of the self that results from Willy's emphasis upon personal attractiveness has been observed by Raymond Williams (*Loman* 15). Willy very much wishes to be the person others desire him to be and has been selling himself for years. His suicide is simply his final commodity exchange. That transaction is prompted by the emotional revelation at the end of act 2 that, as Willy expresses it, "Biff—he likes me!" But this moment of personal, private value is translated almost immediately in Willy's mind over to the hierarchical business realm as he savors the suicide money-making scheme which he joyously exclaims will put Biff "ahead of Bernard again!" (135) Willy here seems to employ traditionally "feminine" means, the commodification of the self, to reach "masculine" ends—being number one man. One remembers his admiration for Biff when he discovers "the girls pay for you?"—a situation that simultaneously involves Biff in a gender role reversal and makes him, in Willy's eyes, a huge success (28).

Willy very definitely exhibits a mixture of typically "masculine" and "feminine" speech and values. This contradictory mixture is evident in his own stated definitions of manhood. On the one hand, he boasts and states unequivocally the qualities a man must exhibit: "A man can't go out the way he came in. . .a man has to add up to something," (125) and "A man who can't handle tools is not a man" (44). On the other hand, he denigrates physical labor saying, "Even your grandfather was better than a carpenter" (61) and asserts, "The man who makes an appearance in the business world, the man who creates personal interest, is the man who gets ahead. Be liked and you will never want" (33). A partial explanation of Willy's mixed aspirations and values may be sought in the sketchy history Miller provides of Willy's childhood. His father, an itinerant flute maker, left the family when Willy was a baby, and his older brother Ben followed suit when Willy was only four. Willy was thus raised by his mother and as a result, he says, still "feels kind of temporary" about himself (51). He expresses his uncertainty about the values he developed to Ben saying, in relation to his own sons, "sometimes I'm afraid I'm not teaching them the right kind of—" (52).

Kay Stanton and Jan Balakian have noted Mother Loman's seeming invisibility in Willy's world (Stanton 68-69; Balakian 120). She appears to have reared Willy alone and yet there are no grand character stories about her in Willy's memories, only mythologized stories of Dad. One wonders about the source of these stories. It is hard to imagine a woman abandoned by both husband and eldest son and left to raise a four year old with apparently no financial help from either one (Ben, when he visits Willy, is unaware that their mother has been dead a long time.) telling glowing stories of her husband. Perhaps the stories come, like much else in Willy's world, only from his imagination, fortified by Ben's few details and projected from Ben's success backward to his father. June Schlueter raises the possibility that Ben himself is Willy's fabrication (148-149), though I tend to credit Ben's existence, if not the enormity of his success. In any case, Willy does seem to have emerged from this fatherless, "feminine" environment with a craving for personal admiration and a talent for self-deception, developed perhaps in response to truths too hard to absorb. His sense of who he should be and how be should behave is a confused mixture of pioneer machismo, belief in the power of personal ingratiation and, it would seem, a genuine desire for love.

Even Willy's relation to Linda in the play, which some critics have seen as frozen into rigid gender roles (Kintz 108), actually shows each of them exhibiting a curious mixture of Tannen's designated "masculine" and "feminine" conversational and behavioral traits with one another. Certainly, Willy frequently dominates their conversations, accusing Linda of interrupting (64) and insisting that she let him talk (when in fact she has not interrupted) until Biff protests angrily, "Don't yell at her, Pop" (65). A moment later, when Linda begins a sentence, the stage directions indicate that Willy interrupts "going right through her speech" (67). Interruptions of this kind and Willy's false perception that Linda is interrupting him match the findings of studies Tannen cites showing that men tend to interrupt women, but perceive women as more talkative than themselves (Tannen 188-89). However, elsewhere in their dialogue one finds Linda taking a conversational role—that of problem solver—that Tannen identifies as typically "masculine" (51-53). Consider the following exchange:

> LINDA: . . . Did something happen, Willy?
> WILLY: No, nothing happened.
> LINDA: You didn't smash the car, did you?
> WILLY, *with casual irritation*: I said nothing happened. Didn't you hear me?

LINDA: Don't you feel well?

WILLY: I'm tired to the death. . . .I couldn't make it. I just couldn't make it, Linda.

LINDA, *very carefully, delicately*: Where were you all day? You look terrible.

WILLY: I got as far as a little above Yonkers. I stopped for a cup of coffee. Maybe it was the coffee.

LINDA: What?

WILLY, *after a pause*: I suddenly couldn't drive anymore. The car kept going off the shoulder, y'know?

LINDA, *helpfully*: Oh. Maybe it was the steering again. I don't think Angelo knows the Studebaker.

WILLY: No, it's me, it's me. Suddenly I realize I'm goin' sixty miles an hour and I don't remember the last five minutes. I'm—I can't seem to—keep my mind to it.

LINDA: Maybe it's your glasses. You never went for your new glasses.

WILLY: No, I see everything. I came back ten miles an hour. It took me nearly four hours from Yonkers.

LINDA, *resigned*: Well, you'll just have to take a rest, Willy, you can't continue this way.

WILLY: I just got back from Florida.

LINDA: But you didn't rest your mind. Your mind is overactive, and the mind is what counts, dear. (12-13)

Here Linda begins by questioning Willy's veracity, and then as he begins to open up and reveal his feelings, rather than responding sympathetically and drawing him out, she begins to suggest further reasons for and solutions to his problems. Though it is true, Willy begins by suggesting bad coffee as a reason for his problems, he rapidly shifts his focus within himself while Linda continues to offer up possible external solutions to his difficulties. Tannen reports this problem-solving conversational behavior to be typically masculine. She finds that for most women telling a problem is a bid for an expression of understanding or mutuality and that women resent men's tendency to respond with offers of solutions (51-53). Here with Willy and Linda we find the typical gender roles reversed as Linda offers a series of solutions while Willy looks within.

Interestingly, when Linda confides to her sons her discovery of Willy's rubber pipe—his provision for suicide—she also describes

Willy and his life's endeavors in a curiously "feminine" fashion. "It sounds so old-fashioned and silly, but I tell you he put his whole life into you and you've turned your back on him" (60). Surely in 1949 it was more usual to speak of an old-fashioned mother as putting her whole life into her children rather than a father. Yet in the Loman family flashbacks it *is* always Willy and his boys who are featured spending time together, though in actuality, given Willy's hours on the road, the majority of the boys' time must have been spent under Linda's supervision. In Willy's own family, as in the family his parents created, though the women may pass more time with the sons, it is the father's input that seems to loom largest.

Gender roles are also atypically aligned in the Loman family when it comes to mathematical ability. Biff's failure in math is a watershed event in the play, redirecting not only his immediate future (he loses his college football scholarship), but precipitating the break in his relationship with his father, since it is while seeking advice from his father about the problem that he discovers Willy's infidelity. But his inability makes him curiously "feminine" and dependent upon the femininely perceived (by Willy) "anemic" Bernard. Even today, male achievement on American standardized math tests has been documented as significantly higher than female achievement, but in the Loman household it is the "anemic," femininely portrayed Bernard and Linda who skillfully handle the math. It is Linda who is always calculating Willy's commission in response to his wild estimates of sales and Linda who is minutely aware of the amount due on all their debts.

Linda is also, simultaneously, treated as a stereotypical "weaker vessel" who needs to be shielded from harsh realities by the men of the play on many occasions. When Willy has been fired and is pressing Biff concerning his appointment with Bill Oliver, he makes shielding of Linda his excuse saying, "I'm looking for a little good news to tell your mother, because the woman has waited and the woman has suffered" (107). While this is true, it is not Linda who needs the good news. Similarly, when he presents his suicide scheme to Ben in his imagination, although he envisions the resulting insurance money going to Biff and not Linda, he still makes her the cause: "Cause the woman has suffered, Ben, the woman has suffered. You understand me?" (125). Biff, too, when Willy is talking aloud to himself about events of the past, shows concern that Linda not know, exclaiming, "Doesn't he know Mom can hear that?" (26) But she has known for a long time. It is Linda who has uncovered the silent testimony of the gas hose attachment and while she shows it to her sons, she ironically feels she must shield Willy from her knowledge of him. She thus clearly contributes to Willy's view of herself as someone who is unaware of the extent of his failure and must be protected from such knowledge. All of this shielding of one another in the family seems in many instances really to be self-protection and surely an example of what Biff means when he says, "We never told the truth for ten minutes in this house" (131).

With regard to the gender issues of truth-telling and truth-shielding, Willy gives interesting advice to the young Biff. He cautions, "Be careful with those girls, Biff, that's all. Don't make any promises. No promises of any kind. Because a girl, y'know, they always believe what you tell them . . ." (27). The advice is meant both to shield Biff from trouble and to shield the girls, but it reveals two interesting operating assumptions. One is that whatever promises Biff might make would be untrue and the other is that girls believe everything boys tell them. One wonders who his models are for this dictum—his father and mother, Linda and himself? He certainly seems to believe that Linda is unaware that Charlie has been loaning him his salary. In any case, he presents a view of men as always deceiving and women as always vulnerable to deception, but also perhaps capable of making trouble by calling men on their promises—like the woman in his hotel room in Boston who insists on receiving her promised stockings (119). Her insistence and refusal to disappear foil Willy's attempt to deceive Biff about his marital infidelity, so that her actions are central to the plot. As a character in the play, however, she barely exists. Though she asserts to Willy's evident pleasure that she "picked" him, not he her (38), their sexual exchange follows a traditional gender pattern—she offers sex in return for economic gain (in this case, stockings), and Willy feels he can evict her at will.

The basic unimportance of women in this play to the central thoughts and action of the characters is startling. As Austin, Stanton and Balakian have observed, women's role in the work is primarily to provide men with what they need, whether it be sex, children, power over other men, or simply convenient scapegoats. Mother Loman is entirely absent. Ben's wife, who produces seven sons and manages to outlive Ben, has no individual presence in the play. Linda, who Willy at one point calls his "foundation and support," (18) is not invited to the men's celebratory dinner, and Biff observes at one point that Willy "always wiped the floor with [her]" (55). Indeed, as Barbara Lounsberry points out, even the furniture in the stage directions—"a kitchen table with three chairs" rather than four seems to leave Linda out. In addition, both Willy and Biff attempt to use female receptionists and secretaries to reach the more powerful men behind them, and Happy continually boasts that he will provide women for Biff, any kind and any time he wants. As Eve Kosofsky Sedgwick has demonstrated in her theory of "male homosocial desire," women in these sorts of interactions are exchanged among men to facilitate men's relation with each other. The women themselves are incidental. As Happy observes about the executives' fiancées he sleeps with, "I don't want the girl, and, still, I take it. . .maybe I just have an overdeveloped sense of competition or something" (25). These women also become Happy's scapegoats—he can't marry because they demonstrate that there are no "good" women except Linda. But Linda too, he thinks, can be appeased by a superficial offering of roses to make up for bad behavior.

The absence of women as active subjects in the play has made the high regard with which the play is held in the American canon problematic for feminist critics. As Austin has observed, the lack of a daughter in this quintessential two son family leaves only the role of wife, mother, girlfriend or secretary for women to portray and makes the weight of attention fall on the male characters' interrelationships (61). Miller's original title for the work—*The Inside of His Head*—certainly seems to indicate that characters loom only as large in the play as they do in Willy's mind. Linda's role is secondary and supportive. She doesn't talk about herself or her feelings, only about the men of the play and their attitudes and actions. Though at least one critic comments on "the depth of her own failure to understand the man she has loved" (Bigsby 89), in a tone that suggests that she has terribly and pathetically missed her purpose in life, no one asks if Willy has understood her. It is not one of his objectives nor a focus of the play. As Miller himself observes, "My women characters are of necessity auxiliaries to the action, which is carried by male characters. . ." (Roudane 370). Indeed, as Schlueter notes, we rely for the version we are given of the Linda of the past entirely upon Willy's remembered reconstruction of her attitudes and remarks.

But while it is true men dominate the play, it is also true, as I have been documenting, that a good measure of the concerns, values and expressions of the chief male character may be termed typically "feminine," according to Tannen's study. Indeed I suggest the critical controversy that swirls around the character of Willy Loman is, in part, generated by the tension between the "masculine" and "feminine" components Miller has given to him—his conflation of the private and the business world, the importance to him of personal relationships and one-up-manship, his desire to be loved and to be "number one." This is not to say that because Willy's espoused values of appearance, charm and personal relations may be labeled "feminine" that they are not also superficial. Willy's interest in being "well-liked," in linking the private and the public, in making and sustaining connections has not produced in his life the kind of close relations women with this focus would typically expect. Ironically, this espouser of connections has very few connections in his private or public life—none with mother, father, brother or brother's family, only sporadic, tumultuous ones with his sons, none in the business community but with his neighbor Charlie and with his wife, a relation based upon fantasies both avoid confronting. So he is, in a sense, a failure in this respect also. But it is not his failure in this area that has produced negative critical views of him—no critics berate him for not having influential friends. It is not his failure to succeed, but, I assert, the curiously androgynous nature of his goals and methods that add fuel to critics' dispute over his right to the title of American Everyman.

Several critics do suggest that uniting the private and public domain could be beneficial and might produce a more humane society, and Balakian offers up Charlie as a possible representative of feminized capitalism (a businessman with compassion who still turns a profit) (124). But the union of the two domains remains, on the practical level, an unrealized ideal. As Tannen has noted, linguistically speaking, the public domain is still male-dominated and women consequently sometimes experience difficulty because their conversational patterns and focus on personal relations and solidarity may be misunderstood or falsely assessed in the workplace. Simply speaking and behaving conversationally as a man, however, is not a successful remedy; for, as Tannen observes, women who talk like men in the workplace are not judged as men would be, they are judged differently and harshly (Tannen 188). I suggest that in Willy Loman's case we have evidence that the reverse is also true. Willy's continual talk of the importance of appearance, charm and friends to

success has elicited harsh judgments from critics unused to finding
such sentiments on masculine lips.

Works Cited

Austin, Gayle. "The Exchange of Women and Male Homosocial
    Desire in Arthur Miller's *Death of a Salesman* and Lillian Hellman's
    Another Part of the Forest." *Feminist Rereadings of Modern
    American Drama.* Ed. June Schleuter. Rutherford: Farleigh
    Dickinson UP, 1989.
Balakian, Jan. "Beyond the Male Locker Room: *Death of a Salesman*
    from a Feminist Perspective." *Approaches to Teaching Miller's
    Death of a Salesman.* Ed. Matthew C. Roudane. New York: MLA,
    1995.
Bigsby, C.W.E. *Modern American Drama, 1945-1990.* Cambridge:
    Cambridge UP, 1992.
Bloom, Harold. "Introduction." *Willy Loman.* Ed. Harold Bloom.
    New York: Chelsea House, 1991.
Blumberg, Paul. "Work as Alienation in the Plays of Arthur Miller."
    Arthur Miller: New Perspectives. Ed. Robert A. Martin.
    Englewood Cliffs: Prentice-Hall, 1982.
Driver, Tom F. "Strength and Weakness in Arthur Miller."
    Arthur Miller. Ed. Harold Bloom. New York: Chelsea House,
    1987.
Kintz, Linda. "The Sociosymbolic Work of Family in *Death of a
    Salesman.*" *Approaches to Teaching Miller's Death of a Salesman.*
    Ed. Matthew C. Roudane. New York: MLA, 1995.
Lawrence, Stephen A. "The Right Dream in Miller's *Death of a Salesman.*"
    Twentieth Century Interpretations of Death of a Salesman. Ed. Helene
    Wickham Koon. Englewood Cliffs: Prentice-Hall, 1983.
Lounsberry, Barbara. "'The Woods Are Burning': Expressionism in
    Death of a Salesman." *Approaches to Teaching Miller's Death of a
    Salesman.* Ed. Matthew C. Roudane. New York: MLA, 1995.
Miller, Arthur. *Death of a Salesman.* New York: Viking, 1967,
    c1949.
Overland, Orm. "Arthur Miller's Struggle with Dramatic Form."
    Arthur Miller. Ed. Harold Bloom. New York: Chelsea House,
    1987.
Roudane, Matthew C. *Conversations with Arthur Miller.* Jackson:

UP of Mississippi, 1987.

Schlueter, June. "Re-membering Willy's Past: Introducing Postmodern Concerns through *Death of a Salesman*." *Approaches to Teaching Death of a Salesman.* Ed. Matthew C. Roudane. New York: MLA, 1995.

Sedgwick, Eve Kosofsky. *Between Men: English Literature and Male Homosocial Desire.* New York: Columbia UP, 1985.

Stanton, Kay. "Women and the American Dream of *Death of a Salesman*." *Feminist Rereadings of Modern American Drama.* Ed. June Schlueter. Rutherford: Fairleigh Dickinson UP, 1989.

Tannen, Deborah. *You Just Don't Understand: Women and Men in Conversation.* New York: Ballantine, 1990.

Wilson, Robert N. "The Salesman and Society." *Willy Loman.* Ed. Harold Bloom. New York: Chelsea House, 1991.

Willy Loman: The Tension Between Marxism and Capitalism

George P. Castellitto

If the tragedy of Willy Loman in *Death of A Salesman* is merely the outcome of the conflict between his inner selves and his many-sided persona and if the dramatic rhythm of the play revolves around Willy's inability to distinguish between his inner world and external reality (Hadomi 157), then the play becomes no more than an expressionistic and allegorical representation of the failure of capitalism and of the ravages that the deterministic materialism of modern capitalist society inflicts on individual consciousness. What Willy experiences throughout the play is the enigma of the tension between Marxist socialism and capitalism; he comprehends that capitalism and its tenets (its several accouterments, its technological devices, its progressive westerly movement to a vanished frontier, its commodity-based philosophical foundation) are both ineffective and inutile. However, despite traditional critical stances that portray Willy as the possibly noble "drummer" whom "nobody dast blame" and who "never knew who he was" (138), Willy does not persist as the failed product of the elusive American Dream but as the man whose unconscious yearnings for the safety of socialism transport him to a point, both metaphysically and psychologically, where the sociological tension between that socialism and the capitalism that Willy has been taught to embrace forces him to the crisis that leads to his suicide. In effect, Willy fails because both socialism and capitalism have failed in the modern world, for neither offers the individual a specific place in the social and metaphysical cosmos that fulfills that individual's needs for financial stability, meaningful relationships, and self actualization. If the Marxist tenet is indeed veridical that "truth" is not eternal but rather conceived institutionally, then the institutional "truth" of Willy Loman's life emanates from the tension between the Marxist socialism that he craves and the capitalist notion of success that inflicts its exacting requirements on his psyche.

In his *Introduction* to the *Collected Plays*, Miller discusses his intentions concerning *Death of a Salesman* in a circuitous manner, continuously shifting his assertions and declaring that the play, originally titled *The Inside of His Head*, is a political, social, and psychological drama about the effects of success on an individual who has failed in the eyes of the system (135-50). Miller discusses briefly the Marxist leanings in *All My Sons* and then declares that "the most decent man in *Salesman* is a capitalist (Charley) whose aims are not different from Willy Loman's" (150). However, there are more salient differences between Willy and Charley than the fact that Willy is a constructor and Charley a lender and giver. Charley acknowledges his dependence on the system of capitalism and attempts to convince Willy of the inscrutable, inescapable, and undeniable economic rationality of working for him rather than consistently borrowing money from him. Willy, however, persists in his refusals to depend on Charley, not because he is the individualistic and independent (though frustrated) product of the American Dream as so many interpretations assert, but rather because Willy mistrusts the tenets of that capitalism whose incisive reality Charley preaches. That reality of capitalism is one that Miller himself condemns in *Timebends*:

> Reality was intolerable, with its permanent armies of the unemployed, the stagnating and defeated spirit of America, the fearful racism everywhere, the waste of everything precious, especially the potential of the young. And if Roosevelt was doubtless on the side of the angels, even he was merely improvising to fend off the day of complete collapse. All that could save us was harsh realism and socialism, production not for profit but for use (71).

William Demastes discusses the parameters of realism in *All My*

Sons, and his assertions concerning the movement from realism to expressionism in that play apply more appropriately to *Salesman* (77); Miller's continual shifts from realistic settings to expressionistic ones manifest two conditions—the failure of the realistic tenets of capitalism and the suppression of the Marxist leanings and ideas in Willy's consciousness.   Willy recognizes that capitalism is the inescapable, realistic, and pervasive veil of the modern world, but that veil has produced a shroud of inconsistent expectations and results, both psychologically and economically.   Therefore, recognizing (at least unconsciously) the Marxist principle that labor is the commodity that has both produced and reduced humanity to its present twentieth-century condition, Willy espouses the doctrine of "being well liked" to indicate his disdain for the possessions that capitalism insists that he must maintain (material effects like his refrigerator and automobile that do not function properly) and to advocate his preference for personal connection with the members of society.   Indeed, Willy is captivated by the notion of family cohesiveness, and his attempt to define the family as a miniature social unit verifies his notion that the capitalist routine of labor that distances him as a salesman from his family is less expedient and desirable than socialist ideals where the individual is adjoined to "other" in the family scenario.

Willy's disdain for the substantive products and isolationist wanderings indigenous to capitalism and his yearnings for the family cohesiveness that existed a decade earlier become the catalysts that propel him from his expressionistic musings to his realistic discernment that capitalism has failed, at least for the needs of his psyche.   Willy's life has been, and continues to be until his suicide, an attempt to produce, and yet his yield has been minimal, slight, frustrating, and elusive.   In his assessment of Marx's socialist doctrine, Louis Althusser in *Pour Marx* asserts that production is the transformative foundation of all social activity; therefore, in the confines of the specific dicta that emanate from capitalist philosophy, Willy's striving for production has been a failure and yet simultaneously an ironic sidling toward a socialist stance in which production does not need to provide financial success but rather render for the producer an association with the individuals in the social unit.   Eric Mottram explains how Miller highlights the "conflict between a man and his society through a system of language which repeats ordinary catch-phrases and shared jargon, manipulated to cover the facts" (29).   *Salesman* employs the habitual language of the

commodity-based consciousness of 1949 to accentuate the prevalence
of production in a capitalist society and to display how, ironically, the
system of capitalist production has failed for Willy, despite the
supposed commonness of both the "things" of that society and of the
language that attempts to denote those things. In a discussion of "the
articulate victims of Arthur Miller," Ruby Cohn indicates that "Willy
is not frugal of words, but he has so few of them that he keeps
repeating his small stock" (79). Thus, the very language that
capitalism produces is itself not only redundant but also insufficient
in its ability to reflect the reality of the failure of capitalism, and that
"linguistic poverty" that Willy exhibits is emblematic of "both the
poverty of his world and the poverty of his dream" (Cohn 75). Willy
himself recognizes the inadequacy of both the system of capitalism
and the commodity-based language that the system employs, for that
capitalistic arrangement concentrates on the production-based assets
of the individual and not on the individual worth of the producer.
The Althusserian notion of the Marxist conception of production
postulates that both individual and collective yield transforms the
individual into a viable and indispensable member of socialist
society; such a view is a credible stance when examining Willy's
dilemma because Willy persists as the almost allegorical embodiment
of failed capitalism and frustrated socialism.

Throughout the play, the commodities purchased in the context of
capitalism (the machines, the objects, the locations) fail to offer to
Willy any enduring and immutable connection with the cosmos and
with others. Besides the Studebaker's and the refrigerator's tenuous
reliability and besides the Loman house being "boxed in" between
"bricks and windows, windows and bricks" (17), the machines
purchased as emblems of apparent capitalistic success fail as well. In
act 2, Howard's recording machine merely rattles off a series of
useless information about the capitals of a sprawling continent that
contains locations but lacks substance. Typical of a product of
capitalism, the recording machine dissipates the family rather than
connects it, for, in Howard's insistence that his wife speak into the
machine, in her unwillingness to do so, and in the maid interrupting
the process, the disassociation inherent in the capitalistic family
joined to each other through acquisition of commodities becomes
apparent. Willy himself does not trust the machine, and, in his
assertion to Howard that he thinks he will get one as well, Willy
expresses his mistrust for the very thing for which he yearns. Indeed,

the "things" of capitalistic production dissect the owner and the assets rather than connect; this sense of separation from self and from other is characteristic of not only Willy but also Biff, the psychological and sociological product of Willy's sermonizing. The individual at the "moment of crisis" (Williams 319) in which he comprehends the inefficacy of the system that has submerged him finds himself finally forced to choose, and it is the impossibility of that choice, a decision Willy has delayed for decades, that forces him to his crisis and to his suicide. Raymond Williams discusses, in his assessment of Joe Keller in *All My Sons*, how the vacillation between choices generates disconnection and the "classical Marxist concept of alienation" (317). Williams further asserts:

> *Death of a Salesman* takes the moment of crisis in which Joe Keller could only feebly express himself, and makes of it the action of the whole play. [T]he guilt of Willy Loman is not a single act, subject to public process, needing complicated grouping and plotting to make it emerge; it is, rather, the consciousness of a whole life (319).

For Willy, that consciousness itself is comprised of a complicated series of contradictory impulses and realistic correspondences in which he simultaneously yearns for and rejects the very items and their accompanying disparities that beckon him both psychologically and socially. This sense of dissimilitude between Willy's longings and his discernment of the fruitlessness of those aspirations affect the diminishing and subsuming of his stature, the loss of his "size" as M. W. Steinberg explains:

> Willy does not gain "size" from the situation. He is seen primarily as the victim of his society; his warped values, the illusions concerning the self he projects, reflect those of his society. His moments of clear self-knowledge are few (86).

In the very act of his diminishment, Willy becomes the emblem of failed capitalism and possible socialism; he is no longer like his brother Ben, the expander and conqueror, but rather he is a miniature unit in a massive construct whose parameters and regulations elude him. In effect, Willy is contained by forces similar to those that suppress John Proctor in *The Crucible*, but Willy is not actually consciously aware of those forces as is Proctor.

Inherent in the suppression of Willy's individuality and the continuance of his dwindling stature is Miller's notion of the contradictoriness of the American myth of the victory of individual consciousness (Kintz 110). If the individual cannot discover connection and personal worth in a commodity-based system, then (Miller is implying) the individual must reject that system and seek another. However, that rejection and that seeking are exactly what Willy is not clearly able to accomplish. Linda Kintz explains that:

> Willy's internalizing of the jumbled myths that surround success point to a particular opposition; the relation between style and substance, a relation that initially presupposes substance but at every turn finds style and appearance to be poised over emptiness (110).

Willy's unconscious leanings dictate to him the manifest emptiness and hollowness of the substantive verities of his existence. Indeed, several critics recognize that Biff's disdain for the pen proceeds naturally as a psychological extension of Willy's contempt for capitalist-based articles that either continuously break down or fail to provide consequential relationships with "other"—the automobile, the refrigerator, the unpredictable recording machine, the stockings that Linda mends and that Willy gives to Miss Francis, the mortgaged home that is now practically empty, the fallow back yard where nothing grows. In both Willy's and the play's unconscious predilection for socialist parameters, Miller is manifesting the failure of the substance of capitalism and displaying the *possibility* of a Socialist consciousness that discerns that submergence in a self-actualizing system where individuals are joined for a type of Althusserian, production-based, transformative, connective existence is preferable to the diminishment of individual stature that occurs in a capitalist system.

In his discussion of the play as "an attack on American institutions and values," Leonard Moss enumerates the several "things" of capitalism that serve as the "sources of corruption" that undermine and eventually destroy Willy: the allure of gadgets that attract and fail, the machismo of American athletic competition, the possession of women as sexual objects, the lack of ethics in business transactions, and the concept of authority and control (Moss quoting from Stallknecht 35-6). *Salesman* is not the first play in which Miller condemns American capitalist practices and the corruption that those customs induce, but Willy is the first character to stand poised on a cliff where the tenets of socialism, however they may be implied within the framework of the play, seem preferable to the principles of the capitalism toward which he strives. Even though Willy comprehends that such a striving is ultimately a gradual progression to his doom, he is compelled to follow the canon of capitalist ideals that he has taught his sons, that has followed him from his youth, that he both despises and covets. The enigma of Willy suspended between the two systems becomes one of the essential and ambivalent elements of the play's capability to allow the reader to apprehend Miller's struggle to reconcile the conflict between a socialism that could prove beneficial and a capitalism that had only proven vituperative.

In his discussion of the McCarthy hearings in his autobiography *Timebends*, Miller expresses his distaste for the phobic capitalists, referring to them as a "tribune of moralistic vote-snatchers" (328) and reveals his sympathy for the proponents of Socialism as individuals who "in their perfectly legitimate idealism had embraced the Russian Revolution as an advance for humanity" (328). Indeed, some of the elements of post-Bolshevik Russia appear as both expressionistic and actual factors in the play's staging. The fallow Loman back yard is reminiscent of the Russian waste land, and the interior set of kitchen and bedrooms is suggestive of the post-revolutionary living quarters assigned to the former aristocracy. Even Willy's dreams and reveries are insubstantial and non-epiphanic, suggesting the Marxist concept of the inefficacy of the spiritual and the religious. The Requiem offers no actual resolution to the conflict between socialism and capitalism, for each speaker advocates an assessment of Willy that neither truly comprehends his ambivalence nor offers a possibility of finality and clarity concerning Willy's social and psychological motives. Thus, the play closes with a confusing and contradictory notion of freedom, and, in Linda's sobbing refrain "We're free" (139), the duplicitous nature of capitalism is once again highlighted. Whether Miller intended *Salesman* to stand as a treatise advocating the possibility of socialism is debatable, and post-structuralist interpretations of the play may only hypothesize about his intentions. The tragedy of Willy Loman is much more complicated than what is contained in Biff's final comment that "the man didn't know who he was" (138). Willy hears the sound of the flute, and in that melody are poised the potentiality of release from the capitalism that engulfs him

and the prospect of epiphany, but Willy cannot and does not choose
to follow that melody, for the throes of capitalism are too pervasive.

Works Cited

Althusser, Louis. *Pour Marx*. Trans. Ben Brewster. Verso Books,
   1965.
Cohn, Ruby. *Dialogue in American Drama*. Indiana UP, 1971.
Demastes, William W. "Miller's Use and Modification of the Realist
   Tradition." *Approaches to Teaching Miller's Death of a Salesman*.
   Ed. Matthew C. Roudane. New York: Modern Language
   Association, 1995, 74-81.
Hadomi, Leah. "Fantasy and Reality: Dramatic Rhythm in *Death of a
   Salesman*." *Modern Drama* 31.2 (June 1988): 157-74.
Kintz, Linda. "The Sociosymbolic Work of Family in *Death of a
   Salesman*." *Approaches to Teaching Miller's* Death of a Salesman.
   Ed. Matthew C. Roudane. New York: Modern Language
   Association, 1995, 102-114.
Miller, Arthur. *The Theater Essays of Arthur Miller*. Ed. Robert A.
   Martin. New York: Viking Press, 1978.
---. *Timebends: A Life*. New York: Harper & Row, 1987.
---. *Death of a Salesman*. New York: Penguin, 1949.
Moss, Leonard. *Arthur Miller*. Boston: Twayne, 1980.
Mottram, Eric. "Arthur Miller: The Development of a Political
   Dramatist in America." *Arthur Miller: A Collection of Critical
   Essays*. Ed. Robert W. Corrigan. Englewood Cliffs: Prentice-Hall,
   1969, 23-57.
Steinberg, M. W. "Arthur Miller and the Idea of Modern Tragedy."
   Arthur Miller: A Collection of Critical Essays. Ed. Robert W.
   Corrigan. Englewood Cliffs: Prentice-Hall, 1969, 81-93.
Williams, Raymond. "The Realism of Arthur Miller." *Arthur Miller:
   Death of a Salesman, Text and Criticism*. Ed. Gerald Weales. New
   York: Viking Press, 313-25.

"It's Brooklyn, I know, but we hunt too": The Image of the Borough in *Death of a Salesman*

Stephen A. Marino

In many interviews, articles, and his autobiography, *Timebends*, Arthur Miller details the importance of his defining experiences in Brooklyn as a boy growing up in the 1920s and 1930s and as a young playwright, husband, and father in the 1940s and early 1950s. Because of the collapse of his coat and suit factory, Miller's father, Isadore, moved his family in 1928, when Arthur was 13, from Manhattan, where they had lived in middle class splendor on East 112th Street in an apartment which Miller describes as "at the edge of Harlem, six stories above the glorious park, from whose windows we could see far downtown, even down to the harbor, it seemed" (*Timebends* 6). The family even had owned a chauffeur-driven seven passenger "National" automobile and a summer bungalow on the beach in Far Rockaway, but the hard times had come for them early, even before the Stock Market crash of 1929. The move to Brooklyn was clearly a step down, and the family relocated to the Midwood section of the borough to a little six-room house on East Third Street where Miller shared a bedroom with his maternal grandfather.

Miller often describes Brooklyn as if it were a rural, frontier outpost, and it certainly must have seemed so to the boy who had lived his thirteen years in Manhattan and to his family whose financial and cultural lives had embraced the city. Miller captures their attitude towards Brooklyn in *The American Clock*, a play which partly chronicles his family's downfall during the depression in the guise of the Baum family. The sisters Rose and Fanny, (characters based on Miller's own mother and aunt), argue over their father's objections to moving to Brooklyn. Fanny says: "And what is he going to do with himself in Brooklyn? He never liked the country" (110). This description of Brooklyn as "the country" typifies an attitude towards the borough in the 1920s and 1930s—a point of view which impressed Miller so much he would later use it in *Death of a Salesman*. For despite the borough's size and population (when Brooklyn joined New York in 1898, it had been the fourth largest city in the country with a population of 1.1 million), surprisingly many areas remained relatively rural even though the infrastructure of the city: streets, trolley, bus, subway and elevated train lines, were being built. And life in an "outer" borough like Brooklyn greatly contrasted with life in Manhattan, what people then (and now) called "the city." As Grandpa says in *The American Clock*: "Brooklyn is full of tomatoes" (111).

Miller's recollections of life in his Brooklyn youth are remarkably consistent in emphasizing the rural and pastoral. In a piece he wrote in 1955 for *Holiday* magazine, "A Boy Grew in Brooklyn," he described the Midwood section thirty years before:

> As a flat forest of great elms through which ran the elevated Culver Line to Coney Island, two and a half miles distant...Children going to school in those days could be watched from the back porch and kept in view for nearly a mile. There were streets, of course, but the few houses had well-trodden trails running out their back doors which connected with each other and must have looked from the air like a cross section of a mole run; these trails were much more used than streets, which were as unpaved as any in the Wild West and just as muddy (54).

In both the *Holiday* piece and *Timebends*, Miller recounts the life of his "two pioneer uncles," Manny Newman and Lee Balsam, both salesman, who had moved their families to Brooklyn after World War I, almost ten years earlier than his own family. Miller describes the Midwood area as "so empty they could watch their kids walking all the dozen blocks to the school across the scrubby flatlands"

(*Timebends* 121). Miller also was aware how greatly his relatives' lifestyle contrasted with his own:

> In the twenties, when the Millers came out from Manhattan in their limousine to visit, the Newsam-Balsam connected houses were flanked by only four other pairs, a line of little wooden homes with flat roofs and three-step stoops surrounded by open flatland where tall elms grew, and wild roses and ferns, and the grass was crisscrossed with footpaths that people used instead of the unpaved streets without sidewalks. With no stores closer than a couple of miles, they bought potatoes by the hundred-pound sack and canned the tomatoes they grew, and their basements smelled hauntingly of earth, unlike Manhattan basements with their taint of cat and rat and urine (*Timebends* 121).

In *Holiday*, Miller also tells how the families kept rabbits and chickens and hunted squirrels and other small game.

Miller is concerned particularly with the physical change of Brooklyn in the era between the world wars, when he witnessed the borough's quick and dramatic change to the wholly urban environment of today. Miller recalls how as the nation and Brooklyn mired in the Great Depression:

> Inevitable changes had helped to destroy so much that was human and lovely in my neighborhood...The woods were gone now and there were houses everywhere and even the last lot left to play football on was turned into a fenced-in junk yard. Bars had begun to sprout along Gravesend Avenue, and the whole idea of drinking, which the old neighborhood had never known became quite normal ....The cars, for one thing, jam bumper to bumper along the curbs on streets where there was so much clear space we could have bumping matches with our first jalopies, and ride backwards and forwards and up on the sidewalks and never find an obstruction anywhere (*Holiday* 122-4).

Miller laments the physical change because to him it signaled a significant change in the human condition:

> It was a village, and the people died like the elms did, and I do not know those who live in their houses now. I go back there now and

then, but whether it is I that am no longer young or people who have changed, I know only that things are alien to me there and I am as strange to the place as I had never known it (*Holiday* 124).

Miller was so influenced by his experiences in Brooklyn that the borough became the prime setting for three of his major plays: *Death of a Salesman, A View From the Bridge*, and *Broken Glass*. He uses the literal settings in Brooklyn as a contrast to other places—both geographic and symbolic. The main characters live in a Brooklyn which is the focal point of a reality with which they are in conflict. In *Death of a Salesman*, Willy Loman's idyllic memory of Brooklyn as an unspoiled wilderness contrasts with the reality of a post-World War II technological culture which has boxed in his wood-framed house with "bricks and windows, windows and bricks." In *A View From the Bridge*, the Sicilian-American society living in the Red Hook section of the borough is consistently connected to its roots in the "Old World" of ancient Italian civilizations. Eddie Carbone succumbs to the same mythic fate as his ancestors. In *Broken Glass*, Sylvia Gellburg, an American Jew living in Brooklyn in 1938, suffers hysterical paralysis because of her concern for the persecution of German Jews during the Holocaust. The play details Sylvia's persecution on this side of the Atlantic by the figurative Nazi in her life: her husband Phillip. Thus, all three plays use physical geography as a metaphor for emotional dislocation.

Brian Robinson has pointed out that one of the main characteristics of modern literature is its use of juxtapositions which rely less on experience in a defined environment and more on fragmentation of experience in settings that may be difficult to define. In many modern texts, the city becomes the geographical locus where the tension between reality and fragmentation of experience is heightened. Despite his reputation as a mere social realist, Arthur Miller has created characters for whom fragmentation of experience results in an emotional dislocation from the reality of the very places in which they live—the Brooklyn depicted in *Death of a Salesman, A View From the Bridge*, and *Broken Glass*.

However, *Death of a Salesman* markedly differs from *A View From the Bridge* and *Broken Glass* in the nature of the main characters' emotional dislocations from the physical settings in Brooklyn. In both *A View From the Bridge* and *Broken Glass*, Eddie Carbone and Sylvia Gellburg physically live in Brooklyn, but are connected to other physical geographic locations. For example, *A View From the Bridge* takes place in the Red Hook section of Brooklyn in the mid-1950s, and Miller sought to place Eddie Carbone squarely in relation to his Sicilian-American immigrant society. However, when Miller first heard in his Brooklyn neighborhood the true tale of Eddie Carbone's desire for his niece and his informing to immigration authorities, he thought he had heard it before as "some re-enactment of a Greek myth." In the writing and production of both the one act and two act versions, Miller created a character, the lawyer Alfieri whose speeches to the audience directly connect Eddie to what Miller sees as the mythic level of the play: Eddie's destiny to enact tragic action. Therefore, many of Alfieri's speeches connect Eddie with his mythic fate, not in Brooklyn, but across the sea in Italy. Alfieri uses the images of the tide, the sea, and blood to connect the Brooklyn immigrant society of the play to its savage roots in Sicily.

But the savagery of ancient civilizations seemingly has been transformed in the new world of Brooklyn. Still, Alfieri witnesses how every few years the refinement of the new world is lost when the ancient, bloody savagery rises again. He makes a series of parallels between the old and new worlds: the green sea of the New York harbor echoes the Adriatic; the circling pigeons of the poor immigrants transform into the falcons and eagles of the ancient world. Moreover, Eddie's savagery parallels the old world savagery. Therefore, the "bridge" of the play's title makes the connection. From the Brooklyn Bridge, one can literally see all the docks on which Eddie works as a longshoremen. However, the metaphoric view extends beyond the breakwater, for Eddie's destiny comes from across the sea, the destiny of his ancestors spans the bridge between the old and new world.

Similarly, in *Broken Glass*, Miller uses Brooklyn as a literal setting from which the characters connect emotionally to another physical place. The play focuses on the cause of Sylvia Gellburg's paralysis: her hysteria about the persecution of Jews in Germany in 1938. However, paralysis works on literal and figurative levels in the play: Sylvia's literal paralysis is symptomatic of an emotional and sexual paralysis between her and her husband, Phillip. Phillip and Sylvia Gellburg's emotional paralysis is connected consistently to the crucial "broken glass" image, and the image forces us to jump back and forth from the literal setting in Brooklyn to events occurring across the sea. Of course, Sylvia's anxiety ostensibly refers to "Kristallnacht"—the night of glass—the literal smashing of the stores and synagogues in Germany in 1938 which began the Nazi pogrom against the Jews. However, the play clearly parallels Sylvia's paralysis over the persecution of Jews with the paralysis in her marriage.   Sylvia and Phillip's marriage is clearly as shattered as glass, and the play ultimately depicts Phillip as the cause of Sylvia's paralysis and the destruction of their marriage. For he is capable of Nazi-like violence as the play often depicts and he actually is the figurative German she fears.   Sylvia ultimately recognizes the connection between her anxiety over the affairs in Germany and her anxiety over her marriage. In fact, she blatantly connects the torture of German Jews with her own torment in Brooklyn.

Death of Salesman uses emotional dislocation from Brooklyn quite differently. For although Willy Loman physically lives in Brooklyn, he does not, like Eddie Carbone and Sylvia Gellburg, connect to a physical geographic location far from Brooklyn. Even though he is a traveling salesman, the center of his physical world is Brooklyn, but more importantly the center of his fragile emotional existence is Brooklyn, too—the Brooklyn of the present and the Brooklyn of the past.   Thus, for Willy, Brooklyn becomes the place of conflict between reality and fragmentation of experience.

Certainly the dramatic tension at the heart of *Death of a Salesman* is Willy Loman's inability to no longer differentiate between reality and illusion. The play depicts the last day in the life of Loman who for thirty six years as a traveling salesman has fought to achieve the material success and personal satisfaction which the American Dream promises, and the play captures the dramatic moments when Willy confronts his failure to achieve them. Willy increasingly escapes the reality of his failure in reveries of the past so that he often cannot differentiate between reality and illusion. In fact, from early in the play, Willy's lament for the Brooklyn of the past is inextricably tied into his conflict between reality and illusion. In the very first scene, Willy complains about the physical changes in Brooklyn over the years:

> The street is lined with cars. There's not a breath of fresh air in the neighborhood. The grass don't grow any more, you can't raise a carrot in the back yard. They should've had a law against apartment houses. Remember those two beautiful elms trees out there? When Biff and I hung the swing between them? (17)

These elm trees exist in the Brooklyn of Willy's past, a Brooklyn which does not exist anymore. More importantly, they exist in the "imaginings" of Willy's mind, the place where the more important dramatic action of the play takes place. Miller's working title for *Death of a Salesman* was *The Inside of His Head*, and certainly, Willy's internal longing for the Brooklyn of the past illustrates how dreaming and illusion works in his mind. Willy longs for an idyllic past, a world when his sons Biff and Hap were young, when Willy thought himself a hot-shot salesman, when Brooklyn seemed an unspoiled wilderness. However, the beautiful elms have been cut down and replaced by apartment houses which signify the reality from which Willy escapes in his imaginings. Willy's wistful longing for the Brooklyn trees includes his complaint about how the "bricks and windows, windows and bricks" (17) have boxed in his house. These buildings represent a modern post-World War II technological culture which encroaches not only on Willy's house, but the very fabric of his existence. Willy longs for a place which does not exist in post-World War II Brooklyn, but only in the memory inside his head.

Thus, in *Death of a Salesman*, Miller transformed his own perception of the physical change of the two Brooklyns he had known into Willy's perception: the Brooklyn in Willy's mind—the pastoral, romantic, unspoiled wilderness; and the Brooklyn of the present time of the play—the place where the apartment buildings of the city loom over the smaller wood frame houses. This contrast between Brooklyn as city and country touches upon many of the conflicts among Willy, Biff, and Hap.

Kay Stanton has described Willy's concern with the pastoral as part of what she calls the "Green World" of the play, one of three competing dimensions (the others being the "Business World" and the "Home," both in the city), which define the masculinity of the American Dream upon which the play is based and in which Willy struggles to define himself and his sons (67). For Stanton, this Green World is defined by the "outdoor" imagery that is scattered in the play: Willy's trees, Ben's jungle, Biff's farms. The outdoors is clearly at odds with the competing dimensions of the city, and neither Willy, Biff, and Hap are sure in which dimension he can best achieve the American Dream. Willy has chosen the Business World, but his continual longing for the "lilacs and wisteria" indicates his regret and confusion at the reality of his choice.

This tension between the city and country is evident in Biff and Hap's illusions, too. Both men dream of financial success and personal contentment, but their conversations clearly reveal they are as confused as Willy on how to achieve them. Hap and Biff often detail their relative disappointment in what they have accomplished in life: Biff torn between his love of outdoors and disdain for the city; Hap stuck selling in a department store. Biff admittedly is "mixed up very bad" (23) about his attitude toward the country and the city. He would like to be out West in the outdoors, but he is torn by not being in business in the city where "I oughta be making my future" (22). Yet he equally abhors the "measly manner of existence" in the city epitomized by riding on "that subway on the hot mornings in the summer" (22). He even declares that he and Hap "don't belong in this nuthouse of a city" (61). Hap is attracted to Biff's suggestion that they buy a ranch, but needs to prove to "those pompous, self-important executives" that he "can make the grade" (24) in his department store located in the city.

Perhaps the most significant contrast between the city and country is evident in the figure of Ben. Willy's oldest brother clearly functions in the play as a symbol of economic success in contrast to Willy's economic failure. A significant part of Willy's emotional struggle derives from his regret at having passed up the opportunity to pursue the rugged, pioneer lifestyle of Ben in the Alaskan frontier and the jungles of Africa. Ben has achieved the American dream by becoming, in Willy's mind, the archetypal hero of the frontier myth with his own diamond mines, his own spread of land, his own economic empire. In contrast, Willy has chosen to stay in Brooklyn and struggles to achieve economic success. In the imagining of Ben's visit to Brooklyn in act 1, Willy attempts to justify to Ben his career as a salesman and his "rugged, well liked, all-around" upbringing of the boys in the city. But Ben makes it clear that Willy has not prepared his boys for success when Ben bests Biff in a mock fist fight by tripping him with his umbrella and saying:

> Never fight fair with a stranger, boy. You'll never get out of the jungle that way (49).

Of course, the jungle here is entirely metaphoric. Willy has not conditioned Biff, Hap, or himself for any fight—fair or unfair—in the larger figurative "jungle" of the play: the workplace of the city in the American economic system.

And Ben shows nothing but disdain for Willy's choice. As he prepares to leave the Loman's Brooklyn home to catch his boat for Africa, he says to Willy:

> And good luck with your—what do you do?
> WILLY: Selling.
> BEN: Yes. Well...He raises his hand in farewell to all.
> WILLY: No Ben, I don't want you to think...(*He takes Ben's arm to show him.*) It's Brooklyn, I know, but we hunt too.
> BEN: Really, now.
> WILLY: Oh, sure, there's snakes and rabbits and—that's why I moved out here. Why Biff can fell any one of these trees in no time! Boys! Go right over to where they're building the apartment house and get some sand. We're gonna rebuild the entire front stoop right now! Watch this, Ben! (83)

These lines reveal the depth of Willy's emotional dislocation. He desires to prove to Ben that Brooklyn is a wilderness where men can hunt and fell trees, where one can succeed on physical abilities. Willy fails to realize that the physical training of his boys with their hands and bodies—making them the finest specimens—gives them skills for the wrong playing field.   For these skills are mostly unnecessary for success in the city, the field and jungle of the Loman competition.

In the recollection of Ben's second visit to Brooklyn in act 2, the contrast between the city and frontier is underscored:

> WILLY: Ben, nothing's working out. I don't know what to do.
> BEN: Now, look here, William. I've bought timberland in Alaska and I need a man to look after things for me.
> WILLY: God, timberland! Me and my boys in those grand outdoors!
> BEN: You've a new continent at your doorstep, William. Get out of these cities, they're full of talk and time payments and courts of law. Screw on your fists and you can fight for a fortune up there (85).

The timberland connotes the frontier origins of America in the eighteenth and nineteenth centuries when the promises and opportunities of a new continent lay for anyone willing to take it. Of

course, Willy regrets passing up the opportunity to make his riches in
the frontier. Ben's line: "Screw on your fists and you can fight for a
fortune up there!" is a figurative evocation of the competitive spirit of
American enterprise at which Ben has succeeded and in which he
invites Willy to partake. However, this scene is merely Willy's
recollection of a chance which he refused.

Of course, the frontier ultimately suggests another level of meaning,
for the "new continent" which awaits Willy has nothing to do with his
life in Brooklyn, the wilds of Alaska, or the jungles of Africa, but
rather the frontier of death to which Ben lures him with a diamond at
the end of the play.

Ultimately, the tension between the city and country is never
resolved in the play. Even Requiem provides no definite insight.
After Willy's burial, Biff is presumably returning to the West and
even asks Hap to come with him. However, Hap declares his
intention of "staying right in this city," where he is "gonna beat this
racket!" (138). Perhaps Miller purposely left this tension. For after
fifty years, we still wonder what legacy Willy has passed on to his
sons—and how does his pursuit of the American Dream translate to
us eking out our existence and creating our own dreams and illusions
in whatever Brooklyn, or city, or suburb, or country we live in?

And perhaps Miller himself has still not resolved the issue for his
own life, for he recently said in an interview: "I've lived half my life
in the country and I am still astounded that this is the case. I keep
thinking I'll get back to the city where everything is happening"
(*Arthur Miller: An Interview*).

Works Cited

Bewley, Marius. "Scott Fitzgerald and the Collapse of the American
    Dream." *The Eccentric Design, Form in the Classic American Novel.*
    New York: Columbia University Press, 1959.
Carpenter, Frederic I. *American Literature and the Dream.* New York:
    Philosophical Library, Inc., 1955.
Ferguson, Alfred R. "The Tragedy of The American Dream in *Death of a
    Salesman.*" *Thought: A Review of Culture and Idea.* 53 (1978): 83-98.
Martin, Robert A. "Introduction." *The Theatre Essays of Arthur Miller.* Ed.
    Robert A. Martin. New York: Viking, 1978.

---. and Steven R. Centola, eds.. *The Theatre Essays of Arthur Miller*. New York: Da Capo Press, 1996.

Miller, Arthur. "A Boy Grew in Brooklyn." *Holiday* 17 (March 1955) 54+.

---. *Arthur Miller: An Interview*. A BBC Production, Films for the Humanities and Sciences, FFH 7295, 1997.

---. *Arthur Miller's Collected Plays*. New York: Viking, 1957.

---. *Arthur Miller's Collected Plays*, Volume 2. New York: Viking, 1981.

---. *Arthur Miller Death of a Salesman, Text and Criticism*. Ed. Gerald Weales. New York: Penguin Books, 1967.

---. *A View from the Bridge* (with *A Memory of Two Mondays*). New York: Viking Press, 1955.

---. *A View from the Bridge* (Two Act Version). New York: Penguin, 1977.

---. *Broken Glass*. New York: Penguin, 1994.

---. *Introduction* to the *Collected Plays*. *The Theatre Essays of Arthur Miller*. Ed. Robert A. Martin. New York: Viking, 1978.

---. "On Social Plays." *The Theatre Essays of Arthur Miller*. Ed. Robert A. Martin. New York: Viking, 1978.

---. *The Theatre Essays of Arthur Miller*. Ed. Robert A. Martin. New York: Viking, 1978.

---. *Timebends, A Life*. New York: Grove Press, 1987.

Richards, David. "A Paralysis Points to Spiritual and Social Ills." *New York Times* 25 April 1994: C11-13.

Robinson, Brian. "The Geography of a Crossroads: Modernism, Surrealism, and Geography." *Geography and Literature: A Meeting of the Disciplines*. Eds. William E. Mallory and Paul Simpson-Housely. Syracuse, N.Y.: Syracuse University Press, 1987.

Stanton, Kay. "Women and the American Dream of *Death of a Salesman*." *Feminist Readings of Modern American Drama*. Ed. June Schlueter. London and Toronto: Associated University Presses, 1989.

From Loman to Lyman:
The Salesman Forty Years On

Susan C. W. Abbotson

John Shockley describes Willy Loman as the "Reagan prototype" due to him sharing former President Reagan's evident belief in the "capitalist-consumerist-get-rich-and-be-well-liked-dream," and for understanding of the "need for selective perception" (53) to keep that dream alive. Both Loman and Reagan are salesman, selling the materialistic American dream of wealth and success by denying "basic points of reality in order to believe in the dream" (49). Personal family problems and glaring evidence of the negative effects of their philosophy are uniformly ignored or adulterated to assume a positive spin. Their view of "facts" is "entirely utilitarian," in service to their ideology of the American dream (50). But Shockley admits that there is an intrinsic difference: "Ronald Reagan, in sum, was what Willy Loman wanted to be: well-liked, at least in a superficial way; entertaining without being a bore; successful; handsome; and not fat" (52). It is noticeable that there is no such discrepancy between Reagan and Lyman Felt, the main character of *The Ride Down Mt. Morgan*.

Whether we deal with the original 1991 London production or the altered American version, first premiered at Williamstown in 1996, *Ride* remains a play which addresses the extreme difficulties of living in an amoral, chaotic postmodern society. Miller tells Jeffrey Borak that the changes he made to *Ride* for the Williamstown production (and subsequent Broadway opening) were "Little things. . .that turn out to be important; relatively minor adjustments; things I didn't have time to do in London" (B4). Miller has streamlined certain aspects of the play to try and make his message clearer, but it is, essentially, the same play.

The Ride Down Mt. Morgan purportedly takes place in the hospital room of a bedridden Lyman Felt who is recovering from a bad car accident. Lyman, we soon discover, is a bigamist, and both of his wives, Theo and Leah, turn up, each unaware, until now, that the other existed. Refusing to accept that he has done anything really wrong, Lyman tries to salvage the situation and keep both of his wives happy. He largely fails in this attempt as it is clearly too selfishly motivated, something his daughter, Bessie, tries to teach him. He ends the play alone; even his admiring friend Tom cannot continue to support his actions.

Ride is an evocation of life in America in the eighties, under the duplicitous and often contradictory leadership of a former movie star. The importance of Reaganism to this play has been recognized by a number of critics. June Schlueter suggests that *Ride* may be read "as a document of the moral narcissism of the Reagan years" (143), and Ben Brantley sees the play as clearly "about the Reagan years, and their voracious consumerism . . . images of bottomless appetite are everywhere" (C16). Lyman's marriage to Leah occurs in the same year that Ronald Reagan became president, and Lyman's bigamous behavior becomes a reflection of the values and type of leadership America subsequently experienced.

It is clear from Shockley's descriptions of Reagan, that Lyman Felt makes a closer comparison to Reagan than Willy Loman. Shockley's Reagan creates a mythic self which, unlike Willy, he *successfully* markets, and Reagan succeeds "not in spite but because of all his paradoxes and contradictions" (53); so, too, does Lyman. Shockley points to the ambivalence between the private reality of Reagan's father's destructive alcoholism and Reagan's public description of his father as a skilled raconteur; Lyman suppresses his private disgust at his father's coarseness and meanness and emphasizes to others his father's strong sense of life. Willy, on the other hand, may mythologize his father into an archetypal pioneer/travelling peddler, but we are given no private sense of what his father was really like to contrast with this image. In addition, Lyman, like Reagan in his dealings with the MCA bribery hearings or the Iran-Contra scheme, escapes an apparent complicity with dirty dealings by informing on others and assuming a veneer of innocence. Willy's dirty dealings— an adulterous affair, allowing his sons to steal lumber—are on a totally different scale, and Willy cannot escape his guilt in these matters. Lyman also, unlike Willy who tends towards boorishness, but like the entertaining President, can be genuinely charming and able to persuade people to admire him. Both Lyman and Reagan possess a stronger sense of self-confidence than Willy is ever able to employ, partly because neither has ever had to face the ignominy of impending failure. Each has been better suited to play the capitalistic game, partly by their more resistant personalities, and partly by their greater ability to find scapegoats to deflect their own responsibilities. But it is not that Miller is asking us to denounce Lyman/Reagan, anymore than he asks us to denounce Willy, what he does ask us is to consider the implications of their behavior.

Shockley's article, however, helps to point us toward the undeniable fact that *Ride* is "signifying" on *Salesman*, just as Chris Bigsby suggests (*British* 25). The similarity between the names Loman and Lyman can hardly be coincidental. Indeed, it suggests that Loman may not so much be a prototype for Reagan, but the prototype for Lyman. While Loman was a man striving against the difficulties of living inherent during the forties and fifties, Lyman is a man for the eighties, and unlike Loman, a very successful businessman. In *Timebends*, Miller relates how he believes he chose the name Loman from a subconscious memory of a scene in the film, *The Testament of Dr. Mabuse*, where a doomed character cries out "Lohmann." "What the name really meant to me," Miller tells us, "was a terror-stricken man calling into the void for help that will never come" (179). But Loman's name has inevitably tended to evoke discussion of Willy as a "low-man" in terms of his abilities, character, or prospects, while Lyman's name, on the other hand, with its possibilities of outrageous deceit (lies), passion (to lie with), and, as June Schlueter suggests, the concept of one who is "lionized" (143), clearly evokes a different sense of being. Where Loman is shown to be powerless, Lyman is fully empowered. Lyman is, what Willy Loman wanted to be, if only he had had that charisma and business sense he so dearly wanted. But we can also see, perhaps even more clearly than *Salesman* informs us, just how misguided Willy's desires were, as we witness the dangerous and unsatisfactory life Lyman has created with all those skills and advantages for which Willy had longed.

Lyman's actual "ride" down, what Hugo Williams calls "Mount More-Gain" (29), is emphasized by the choice of title. The title of the play can be taken as a metaphor for the dizzying experience of life in the eighties—comparable to hurtling down an ice-covered mountain. The last nine years for Lyman, since his earlier encounter with a lion while on safari with Theo and Bessie, have been a metaphorical ride down a steep slope, dangerous and out of control, hurtling towards an inevitable crash. Completing such a run without spinning off is a skill we must learn in order to survive. Perhaps we should see the rise in recent years of perilous, fast moving sports, from rollerblading to snowboarding, as a reflection of this aspect of our contemporary society? Lyman gets somewhat broken in the process of his ride, but he does survive, which should draw our attention to the qualities he possesses which allow for this. Bigsby suggests, that Lyman, with what Miller has called, his "limitless capacity for self-deception and for integrity," becomes an emblem for a contemporary society, which is also "capable of enormous construction and destruction" (*British* 25). We see the ambivalence in such descriptions—Lyman has the capability for greatness, but to both good and evil ends.

Miller clearly wants us to see the deep irony in Lyman's situation—a life-insurance mogul who may have just tried to kill himself, and in a car just like his predecessor, Willy. We are certainly being led to recognize a link between insurance and immortality (or perhaps mortality). Lyman begins the play very disoriented, he's been shaken up, buffeted by the storm which has been raging outside both mentally and physically. This is a time of change for him and we are to learn the circumstances and desires which have necessitated this change. As with Loman, Lyman is a character through whom and through whose actions we are being asked to question a number of the values we have so complacently accepted and lived with, without sufficient understanding. Just like Loman, Lyman too seeks that elusive "main thing;" the secret to life each feels exists but is somehow being kept hidden from them. What neither realizes is that there are sometimes only questions, and answers do not always exist. Their desire for the main thing gives their worlds order, so to face its non-existence is tantamount to destroying the order of their worlds. They must learn to live with this truth, but it is a truth both try to avoid through obsessively recreating scenes on the stage before us, as if by this recreation, their lives can somehow be made to turn out right after all.

While the scenes which spring from Loman's mind are well signposted in *Salesman*, Miller makes it far harder to recognize any reality in *Ride*. As a possible reflection of both the increasingly chaotic times in which Lyman lives, and the sheer strength of Lyman's will, the scenes are no longer just recreations of the past, but also include episodes from the present and the future. We cannot trust our eyes when watching *Ride*; it is impossible to say for sure if any of the encounters or events take place anywhere other than in Lyman's mind. In considering what might be real and what imagined, William Henry even questions the existence of Lyman's illegitimate child and the fact of his encounter with the lion, seeing this latter memory as a "mere metaphor for the kind of masculinity he is trying to keep alive" (101). Bigsby questions if the wives ever really meet (*Modern* 121) and suggests that because of the way they are presented "it is difficult, too, to make definitive judgements on the two women, for if they seem to represent, at times, too clear a polarity, this is in large degree because they are presented to us through the transforming imagination and memory of Lyman" (*Modern* 123). This idea of Lyman's "transforming imagination" would suggest that the play, in one sense, evidences an attempt by Lyman to form order from chaos.

One difficulty audiences had, with the London production particularly, was an inability to distinguish between what was really happening in the play and the imaginary scenarios being dreamed up by Lyman. Even though Miller, to keep his audience happy, makes this switch between apparently real and fantasy events clearer in the American production—the point is, it really is impossible to say for sure if any of the play's events exist outside Lyman's imagination as he lies prone in his hospital bed. Indeed, is Lyman's crash and hospitalization even real, or just the product of a guilty conscience? The discrepancies in fixing Lyman's age may underline this, unless they are merely something Miller overlooked. We are told at the start that Lyman is a man in his fifties, and yet during the play we learn that he turned fifty-four supposedly nine years previously when he married Leah, which would make him sixty-three—Willy's age. So perhaps, his whole bigamous relationship has been a mere figment of his imagination—maybe that lion attacked after all, and it is this earlier accident for which he is now in the hospital?

Opening the play with a man asleep is Miller's way of warning us that this whole play could turn out to be nothing more than one man's dream (or nightmare) with the patient waking, perhaps, only at the close with a strangled cry, or perhaps never waking at all. We are kept deliberately unsure as to what exactly is real and we must pass judgment without the nicety of certainty. In his dreams, at least, we see Lyman able to escape the human limitations of his casts and also, perhaps, the human limitations of his guilt, conscience and sense of responsibility—all of which are troubling him. It seems likely that the whole first act is an extended dream apart from one brief chat with the nurse near the beginning. As Miller explained in an open debate given in Williamstown prior to the opening there of *Ride*, the action of the play should move like "a lyric rather than a drama." This is no slice-of life realism, but an expressionistic evocation of one man's existential dilemma, much as *After the Fall*. Lyman may awake later in act 2 when Tom joins him for a chat (75), but most of the second act drifts in and out of the past making it hard to assess what may be taking place in the here and now. However, the play does seem to end with the present reality of Lyman abandoned by all but the nurse, and essentially alone.

Just as Willy Loman's father was an important influence on his son's psychological make-up, so too is Lyman's father, and this time we even get to see him. Lyman's father appears on stage right at the start of the play to signify his importance in the make-up of this man called Lyman Felt—who tells lies, lies with women and has *felt* the full exhilaration of life—although "felt" is noticeably in the past tense as Lyman has now reached an impasse which needs resolving if he is to continue. But what is it that Lyman must learn—and does he actually learn it during the play? Is it something to do with responsibility—a lesson introduced so peripherally by his own daughter, Bessie—though largely ignored by all present? Lyman's father appears as a figure of both hope and fear; inspiration and intimidation; his memory both encourages and restricts the son. Lyman's Father died at fifty-three—Lyman worries greatly about the state of his life when he reaches the same age, and this is the point when he makes all these strange and daring changes in his life.

June Schlueter's suggestion that Lyman's father is the "contributing author of Lyman's troubled (arguably abusive) relationship with women, who he consistently characterized as sexual objects" (147), rings true. The father's opening speech is fraught with images of restriction which he places on his son: he will not buy Lyman skates, and so restricts his movement (literally and symbolically); he warns him strongly about having anything to do with women, thereby, restricting Lyman's future relationships and ability to connect with women; he criticizes Lyman's looks and abilities, telling him he is "stupid" and a "great disappointment" (2), which must restrict Lyman's intrinsic self-esteem. However, and it is this which makes us most aware of Lyman's great spirit, Lyman has seemingly overcome these restrictions. In the world he inhabits, unlike Willy Loman, Lyman Felt is a great success—a wealthy man with not one, but two, attractive women to show off; he seems to have come a long way from his father's humble origins. But, he is to learn in the course of the play that he has really remained firmly within his father's restrictions and that his success has been a false one—he has not progressed spiritually, he has little connection with either of his women, and he is still desperately seeking his father's approval.

The father's advice to Lyman regarding business and passion fully illustrate his son's inner conflict. Lyman is torn between the practical—the male world his father invokes of cold cash and WASP principles—and the emotional—a female world of sex, recklessness and the Jewish lust for life. The two seem to be at odds, his father demands the first takes precedence, but Lyman needs a balance between the two, as indeed do we all. At least this is what he is striving to gain, although he has to break a number of rules in the process. He is caught between his more primal love for the Jewish Leah and the sexuality she offers, and the regard and admiration he cannot deny for the more reserved, WASPish Theo, a true American lady—he wants a combination of both but that is not so easy to achieve. Lyman can be seen as an exaggerated version of the tension in all of us between right/wrong, clean/dirty, good/evil, and proper/perverse.

Richard Christiansen describes Lyman as "a guilt-filled man faced with a late life domestic crisis" (24) and so reduces him, unnecessarily, to the mundane. It is easy to see the harsher, unpleasant side of Lyman, but the point is, as other critics have pointed out, that there is also a very attractive side to his character. Michael Eck approves strongly of F. Murray Abraham's depiction of Lyman in the Williamstown production as "a complete man—as evil and attractive and as powerful and pathetic as the lines suggest" (D6). John Peter also talks of Lyman's "lethal duality: he is the maker who wants to create and belong but also the cynic who needs to undermine and rebel" and one can view the play as having this same ambivalence. As Peter suggests: "The opening situation is catastrophic or funny, according to your point of view" (7). When Peter Lewis asks Miller if Lyman is supposed to be despicable or interesting, Miller replies: "To me he's both" (6). Miller insists that:

> I can't give people a ready made solution to something so complex. I don't give them a team to root for. You could send them out happy, but they'd only be happy until they stopped to think about it. I decided to leave it in their laps, not so much as a problem but as a life situation (6).

In an on-line interview that Miller gave with *Mr. Showbiz*, he was asked if he saw Lyman as an honest, life-embracing hero, or a self-absorbed jerk; Miller answered:

> I see him as a little of both. He is selling himself that he's embracing life by seeing himself as the main character in the world. The people around him are somewhat lesser in their values. The result is that he's an egoist. What I was getting at is the whole question of letting it hang out: simply expressing one's self regardless of the consequences.

Vision is integral to leading a satisfactory life as it is needed in order to create the better fictions towards which we aim—otherwise we get too enmired in the here and now. Willy's ultimate downfall comes when he lacks sufficient vision to reimagine his own life, and must turn to imagining his son's life instead; Lyman at least has the vision to stay alive, even if he remains somewhat selfish in the process, and certainly more alone than when he started.

We should recognize the subtle contrast to Lyman provided by Nurse Logan at the end of the play. She talks more of her family than of herself, she listens rather than tells. She is satisfied and content with no sign of angst. She doesn't need everything explained/understood; she accepts mystery and is satisfied with *less*, perhaps, but nonetheless is satisfied. In this light, it may be Lyman's ambition which, ironically, has inhibited him? His desire for continued excitement has escalated, as has his need to take greater and greater risks—a fall was inevitable. But in another way we have seen him go full circle. By the end, the commonplace events and concerns described by Logan have become unusual and exciting to Lyman, as he has gone so far from that kind of life it now seems strange and alien to him. Logan has the simpler response to life that was perhaps the same as Lyman's father's—and the resulting contentment Lyman has been seeking. Miller seems to suggest that society is forcing us all to live increasingly complicated lives—but humanly we cannot keep up, and really shouldn't try. As Thoreau said so long ago: "Simplify! Simplify!"

Lyman's final confession seems to be given more to the audience than to Leah as the light fades, to highlight Lyman alone as he describes the similarity between facing that mountain and the lion. "All obligations spent. Is this freedom?" Lyman now asks. He is beginning to realize that freedom is not what he wanted after all. Complete freedom means no connections at all, which is of course awful. He ends the play alone, shaken and sobbing—with only the nurse's evident compassion to mitigate his isolation. But, unlike Willy Loman, Lyman Felt ends alive, which is hopeful he may yet learn. He is also suffering, which can be seen as a positive sign as it implies that he has, finally, acknowledged his connection to others, and has become humanly engaged. We can find hope for his future in that he does seem closer in touch with the simple reality of the Nurse and her family; this may help him recreate his own life against a more reasonable template, and reach that satisfaction with life that he has sought for so long.

Works Cited

Bigsby, C. W. E. "A British View of an American Playwright." In *The Achievement of Arthur Miller.* Ed. Steven R. Centola. Dallas: Contemporary Research, 1995: 17-29.

---. *Modern American Drama 1945-1990.* Cambridge: Cambridge UP, 1992. (*MAD*)

Borak, Jeffrey. "Miller At 80 Fine-Tuning Play's American Performance." *Berkshire Eagle* 4 Jul. 1996: B1, B4.

Brantley, Ben. "Arthur Miller, Still Feeling the Pain After the Fall." *New York Times* 25 Jul. 1996: C13, C16.

Christiansen, Richard. "Arthur Miller Opens New Play in London for Good Reason." *Chicago Tribune* 13 Nov. 1991, sec. 1: 24.

Eck, Michael. "Williamstown Theater Festival's *Mount Morgan* is Pure Arthur Miller." *Times Union* 24 Jul. 1996: D6.

Henry, William A. III. "Arthur Miller, Old Hat at Home, Is a London Hit." *Time* 138 (11 Nov. 1991): 100-01.

Lewis, Peter. "Change of Scene for a Mellow Miller." *Sunday Times* 3 Nov. 1991, sec. 6: 6.

Miller, Arthur. Interview. "Mr. Showbiz Celebrity Lounge Interview." *Starwave*. Online. 10 Jan. 1996.

---. *The Ride Down Mt. Morgan*. Harmondsworth: Penguin, 1992.

---. *Timebends: A Life*. New York: Grove, 1987.

Peter, John. "Rev. of *Ride*." *Sunday Times* 3 Nov. 1991, sec. 6: 7.

Schlueter, June. "Scripting the Closing Scene: Arthur Miller's *Ride Down Mount Morgan*." In *The Achievement of Arthur Miller*. Ed. Steven R. Centola. Dallas: Contemporary Research, 1995: 143-50.

Shockley, John S. "*Death of a Salesman* and American Leadership: Life Imitates Art." *Journal of American Culture* 17 (Sum. 1994): 49-56.

Williams, Hugo. "In Bad Taste." *Times Literary Supplement* 8 Nov. 1991: 29.

A View from *Death of a Salesman*

Jane K. Dominik

The fiftieth anniversary Broadway production of *Death of a Salesman* prompts a retrospective view of an American masterpiece, and provides an opportunity to recognize its continuing universality and its place in twentieth-century drama. The play which launched Miller as a foremost playwright of this century, and the one upon which he believes his reputation will ultimately lie, offers a significant vantage point from which to view common elements that permeate his other twenty-eight plays. If Miller had ceased writing successful plays after 1949, he still would have made his mark. Most criticism centers around this play and a handful of others. A comprehensive examination of his drama, however, reveals his persistent attention to certain themes and characters, even as he has experimented with form, structure, and staging over sixty-three years of playwriting.

Salesman's universal appeal and impact are evident. "Since its premiere, there has never been a time when *Death of a Salesman* was not being performed somewhere in the world" (Murphy 70). The relevance of the play continues due to the widespread influence of a capitalistic system which values increased production and conspicuous consumption.[1] Stories abound over the past fifty years which reveal that Willy is the Everyman of the modern world: men sobbed during the premiere performance in 1949, and audiences gasped in 1999; a young Greek woman's perspective of her older co-workers changed overnight upon reading the play in the '90s, and a young Japanese man stated, "Willy is my father," referring to Japanese business practices and sales quotas pressing upon a traditional sense of honor; upon leaving the theatre in 1949, Bernard Gimbel told his assistant that no one in his department stores "was to be fired for being overage" (Miller, *Timebends* 191), and Chinese actors and audiences in Miller's Beijing production in 1983 had little difficulty in understanding and relating to Willy's dilemmas (Miller, *Beijing* 247).

The universality of *Salesman* across time and culture has endured, resting on major themes which are re-examined and re-shaped in other Miller plays: the mutually-effective relationship between man's social and psychological worlds, and between family and society; the conflict between old and new, rural and urban; the effects of the past upon the present; guilt and denial of responsibility; and reality versus dreams and illusions.

Willy Loman struggles within a web of these thematic dichotomies. He has attempted to succeed in a world contradictory to his values and interests. He yearns for validation by a system which defines success according to sales figures, a substantial income, and social prestige, yet what he enjoys most is working with his hands and being with his family. Willy's professional aspirations are predicated upon his desire to gain his sons' respect, but it is precisely those aspirations which destroy his family.

Willy is alone in his salesman's world, and before he can take his sons on the road with him as promised, he resorts to an affair in Boston to relieve his loneliness, boost his faltering ego, and possibly gain sales. After one of their rendezvous', The Woman promises to put him "right through to the buyers." Biff's image of Willy is shattered in a single, horrifying moment when he discovers his father's adultery and sinks into a disillusionment from which he never recovers, destroying the dreams of both father and son.

The mutual effects of society and family are a prevalent theme in Miller's dramas from the beginning of his work as a playwright. Characters are caught between trying to maintain their homes and their work in a futile situation; if they succeed in one arena, they fail in the other. Miller's earliest plays, written in 1936 and 1937, remain unpublished, and are, in essence, versions of the same story. In *No Villain*, *They Too Arise*, and *The Grass Still Grows*, a strike threatens a father's coat manufacturing business.[2] The family's economic survival depends, of course, on that business, but Miller places the conflict in the center of the family: one son supports the strike, while the other supports his father. In Miller's adaptation of *An Enemy of the People*, Dr. Stockmann sacrifices his status and livelihood as a physician, and, therefore, his family's safety and financial stability, by insisting that the polluted springs are too dangerous for the town's proposed profitable health resort. In *A View from the Bridge*, Eddie Carbone's incestuous desire for his niece leads him to report her fiancé to immigration authorities, thereby becoming an outcast in his Italian immigrant neighborhood. And in *Clara*, the title character's father indirectly causes her murder. His socially liberal ideals prevent him from protesting her choice of boyfriend, an ex-con who killed his previous girlfriend.[3]

In *Salesman*, Willy's struggle between society and family is complicated by his struggle between the old and new, and between rural and urban life. Willy's boss, Frank, has been succeeded by his son Howard, who has little sympathy for an aging, ineffectual salesman. Willy contrasts the two generations: "If old Wagner was alive I'd a been in charge of New York by now! . . .But that boy of his, Howard, he don't appreciate." Willy refuses to acknowledge change, just as Victor and Walter's father in *The Price* failed to cope with financial catastrophe wrought by the Depression. Unable to face a new start, Mr. Franz recreated his former home in miniature by cramming ten rooms of furniture into a single attic room in an effort to retain something of his world which had collapsed.

In earlier times and in old world countries, identity was established more by family name than by accomplishments. Misguided, Willy attempts to succeed by his name in a new world. His primitive utterance toward the end of the play, "I am not a dime a dozen! I am Willy Loman and you are Biff Loman!" is a fundamental plea for significance of individuation, family, pride, and honor. It is a plea also echoed by other Miller protagonists. Joe Keller in *All My Sons* rationalizes his decision to allow faulty airplane parts to be shipped in order to have a business for his son, while in *The Crucible*, John Proctor refuses to allow his false confession of witchcraft to be posted on the church door, crying, "How may I live without my name? I have given you my soul; leave me my name!" And, Eddie Carbone challenges Marco, who has publicly accused him of betrayal: "I want my name, Marco. Now gimme my name. . . ."

Willy is puzzled by the success other sons enjoy: Howard inherits his father's business, and Bernard becomes a lawyer even though Charley "never told him what to do. . .never took any interest in him." Clearly, family retains its importance, but only for those who can play the game. They cannot rely simply on name; they must deliver the goods. But Willy and his sons cannot deliver.

The old and new dichotomy is not only a temporal one; it is a conflict created by the urban world infringing upon, and replacing the rural. Willy abhors the changes time has wrought in his neighborhood: the two beautiful elm trees have been cut down to make way for an apartment building, and his back yard, which used to be filled with lilac, wisteria, peonies, and daffodils, is a place where even grass and carrots cannot grow. He refuses to accept these changes, attempting to plant seeds "in the blue of the night" because "[he doesn't] have a thing in the ground." In infertile soil, he must plant; in a seemingly useless life, he must leave a legacy.

Willy's own father and brother succeeded in the wilderness, but, with Linda's encouragement, Willy remained in the city. While the tremendous success of his brother might be questioned—like other memories which have been enhanced over time—if Ben, indeed, discovered diamonds, it was by dumb luck, not design or intelligence. He headed north for Alaska but ended up "heading due south. . .[and] found him in Africa." Inheriting his father's indecision, Biff fluctuates between city and country, between civilization and the wild. He loves the open air and work on farms out west, but believes he must return home because he is "not getting anywhere." Yet, when he returns, he tells Happy, "And now, I get here, and I don't know what to do with myself. I've always made it a point of not wasting my life, and every time I come back here I know that all I've done is to waste my life." Following in his father's footsteps, upon Willy's suicide, Happy, his younger son, announces that he will continue his father's fight in the urban jungle to "win it for him."

Connections between old and new worlds abound in Miller's drama. The new world offers freedom, the old world provides roots. In *The Golden Years*, Cortez comes to the new world of Mexico in order to conquer Montezuma's ancient Aztec civilization; in *Enemy*, Dr. Stockmann considers sailing to America to escape small town hypocrisy; in *Bridge*, immigrants work to send money back to their families in Italy; in *The Archbishop's Ceiling*, Maya encourages Sigmund to flee eastern Europe to avoid censorship of his manuscript, persecution, and imprisonment; and in *Broken Glass*, Sylvia is paralyzed due, in part, to Kristallnacht three thousand miles away in Europe.[4]

Willy's struggles between family and society, old and new, rural and urban are further amplified by his internal struggle to deny his guilt even as he fears its effects, just as Joe Keller maintains his innocence in a neighborhood complicit with his guilt after a second court trial has exonerated him. Willy continues to dream of a shining past and a glorious future, living in his hopeful—or hopeless— illusions in order to stave off defeat, failure, and resignation. He claims to have "averaged a hundred and seventy dollars a week in the year of 1928" although Linda's figures reveal his exaggeration; he recalls Biff's golden days of high school football and popularity, comparing him with the mythical Adonis; and he assures Biff that Bill Oliver "always liked [him]" when, in truth, Biff has stolen from Oliver, who does not even remember him.

The clash between reality and illusion, often based on idealistic naïveté, is evident throughout Miller's work, from Donna Marina's belief in the benevolent intentions of Cortez until it is too late to stop him, to Victor's loyal and financial support of his father who actually had money saved, to *Mr. Peters' Connections*, Miller's latest play, in which the protagonist questions what is real and what is imagined.[5]

Another thread of conflict which comprises Willy's web of entanglement is the past impinging upon the present. Willy longs for the past, but it is a past which has been romanticized through memory. After he is fired, Willy's illusions and memories of success and familial love are punctured by reality when Biff reports his failure and theft in Bill Oliver's office earlier that day. The past impinging upon the present is a major theme in Miller's work, one for which he has continually sought a form: "The structure of a play is always the story of how the birds came home to roost" (Martin and Centola 179). Numerous protagonists are entrapped by their earlier actions, including John Proctor by his adultery, Victor by his unnecessary sacrifice of a college education, and Sylvia by her willingness to relinquish her dreams to placate her husband.[6]

In *Salesman*, Biff finally forces Willy to face reality. "[Whipping] the rubber tube out" to confront Willy with his suicidal intentions, he exclaims, "We never told the truth for ten minutes in this house!" Biff's challenge echoes Chris Keller's when he learns of his father's guilt: "Now blame the world. Do you understand that letter?" Willy can no longer hold back the dam of evidence. Biff accepts responsibility for his own life: "I'm nothing, Pop.   Can't you understand that? There's no spite in it anymore. I'm just what I am, that's all."   But Willy can accept neither himself nor his son as average.

Other characters throughout Miller's drama, including Joe Keller, John Proctor, Eddie Carbone, and Lyman Felt in *The Ride Down Mt. Morgan* are ultimately forced to face their culpability.[7] The image of the concentration camp tower "dominating the stage" in *After the Fall* reflects Miller's contention that guilt is eternal, haunting, and must be acknowledged.

When Willy must admit his responsibility, his course of action is suicide. He cannot remain in present reality long and retreats into illusion, now to dream of leaving Biff his life insurance money to get started in business. But, if Willy has taught his sons to bully, lie, steal, and womanize, he has left them with a questionable tragic and ineffectual inheritance.   Willy's suicide echoes in Joe Keller and Eddie Carbone upon recognition of their guilt, in John Proctor's desire to retain his honor, and in Von Berg's sacrifice for Le Duc in *Incident at Vichy*. Although Miller has continued his exploration of guilt and responsibility, beginning with *After the Fall*, his protagonists are kept alive to face their guilt and its consequences.[8]

The basic character types in *Death of a Salesman* reappear frequently throughout Miller's other plays. If these are his demons which he has continually sought to understand and purge, they also reverberate with audiences, thereby acquiring universal significance. There will always be men who cannot cope with reality and commit suicide; sons who fail to live up to their fathers' expectations and brothers who compete with each other; unfaithful husbands and loyal wives; antagonistic bosses and friends whose advice is sought but never followed; and characters from people's pasts who continue to haunt them.

Miller frequently places two brothers at the center of his plays. He incorporates the foremost archetypal brothers, Cain and Abel, in *The Creation of the World and Other Business*. In several of his plays, fathers are brothers themselves, as well as having two sons. The two brothers often represent halves of their father. As such, they are split, incomplete, and psychologically impotent.   Their internal conflict results in an external stasis. Often the father seeks admiration from the son who has left home, readily dismissing the more loyal one who has remained. Even if the father has died and does not appear in the play, the split between brothers has already occurred, and the two are left to deal with their conflicts.

In *Salesman*, Willy fantasizes about his older and successful brother Ben, wondering what might have been had he gone with him. But Willy stayed. Biff has inherited his father's ambivalence, unable to stay either away or at home for long. He seeks to compensate for his father's adultery, at times subconsciously attempting to replace Willy. He argues with his father, but loves Linda, referring to her as "my pal." It is interesting to note that Willy refers to his wife as "kid," verbally taking on a paternal role. Although Biff finally tells Linda, "[Willy] always wiped the floor with you." Linda rejects the Oedipal triangle: "You can't just come to see me because I love him."

Happy constantly begs for Willy's attention, but is ignored. He inherits Willy's bragging, fighting, and womanizing. He is determined to succeed in business, but, like Willy, uses inappropriate methods to succeed: "I mean, I can outbox, outrun, and outlift anybody in that store, and I have to take orders from those common, petty sons-of-bitches till I can't stand it any more." Happy has also inherited Willy's delusions of grandeur, which Biff challenges: "You big blow, are you the assistant buyer? You're one of the two assistants to the assistant, aren't you?"

There are numerous pairs of brothers in Miller's other plays. In *Villain*, *Arise*, and *Grass*, Arnold returns from college, supports strikers, and refuses to sacrifice anything for family loyalty, while Ben sacrifices a college education in order to work for his father. In *Arise*, he even agrees to marry the daughter of his father's business rival in order to save the business. In *Sons*, Larry pays for his father's sin by committing suicide in a self-conscious effort of poetic justice; he intentionally fails to return from a mission, dying in the same way as those who were indirect victims of his father's unethical decision. Chris embodies the responsibility Joe must face and rejects his father's implied offer to bequeath the business to him, an offer Joe makes in order to justify and exonerate himself. Dr. Stockmann is pitted against his brother, who, as mayor, is much more interested in his town's fame and economy than the safety of its visitors. In *The Price*, Mr. Franz's own brothers relegated him to the attic when he lost his money. Walter left their father after the Depression in order to become a doctor, while Victor stayed to support him financially and emotionally. Conflicts between brothers can continue even after one of them has died. As Miller writes in his preface to *Mr. Peters'*

Connections: "Calvin. . .is also long dead even if the competition between them is very much alive in Peters' mind." [9] Miller's personal concerns about fraternal relationships are revealed in notes he kept while writing *The Price*, comparing and contrasting Walter with his own brother Kermit.[10]

   Salesman is the earliest play which includes an unfaithful husband, a loyal wife, and a mistress or love interest. Miller's male protagonists who stray, value the security of their wives, yet enjoy the sexual excitement and freedom a mistress or younger love interest offers. They want both, in much the same way they equivocate between old and new, home and frontier. Those wives who learn of their husbands' infidelity remain loyal, but suspicious, putting a permanent strain on the marital relationship. Miller's treatment of mistresses varies: some appear little, if at all in the plays, while others refuse to relinquish the man they have seduced and love.

   Willy refers to Linda as his "foundation" and "support," yet he loves the unbridled attention and appreciation The Woman bestows upon him. Linda never learns about her husband's affair, but she demonstrates her loyalty and love by trying to protect Willy from harsh reality.

   In *The Crucible*, Elizabeth Proctor cannot forgive or forget her husband's one-night stand with Abigail until both she and John have been imprisoned. Elizabeth then echoes Linda's protection of her husband, a lie which ironically seals their fate. In *A View From the Bridge*, Eddie Carbone's desire for his niece, while consummated only with a forced kiss, threatens his marriage. Still, when he has alienated his neighbors and niece, his wife Beatrice stands by him. However, in *Salesman*, *Crucible*, and *Bridge*, it is the protagonists' adultery which ultimately causes their demise and suicide. In *Some Kind of Love Story*, Tom has had a relationship with Angela, who now might hold the key to a case he is investigating to free an innocent man from prison. Although her husband, who beats her, is in the next room, she begs Tom for his attention and company in a myriad of ways. Tom's wife suspects that he is still in love with Angela and is "talkin' separation." In *Morgan*, Lyman's two wives are brought face to face after he has crashed his car. He attempts to understand and rationalize his bigamous desires, but to no avail. Miller's perspective of women characters has shifted in this play, written in 1991. While they both love him, neither remains loyal although Theo, the elder wife, must be urged to leave. In *Broken Glass*, Margaret is suspicious of her husband's relationship with

Sylvia. She urges him to find another doctor to treat Sylvia because of his past infidelities. But Dr. Hyman reminds her that "there's been nobody for at least ten or twelve years." He does not succumb to his attraction to Sylvia although, as he tells her husband, she "is desperate to be loved."[11]

In plays in which professional success is paramount for characters, bosses come to represent a system within which man must struggle and win or be eliminated. In *Salesman*, Willy's boss is his primary antagonist. Willy tries to convince Howard to let him work in New York, claiming a superb sales record. When he loses his temper, Howard fires him, launching Willy's final descent. The strongest similarity to this relationship with an antagonistic boss is Gellburg's relationship with Stanton Case in *Broken Glass*. Like Willy, Gellburg assumes a false *persona* as someone who has connections. Gellburg's confident advice to not purchase a property, acting as if he has inside information, proves incorrect, costing Case desirable real estate. Gellburg loses control, worried that Case suspects him of favoring other Jews in business. In the midst of his second appeal to be trusted, Gellburg suffers a heart attack. Similar to Willy, his confrontation with his boss is the beginning of his end.[12]

With the world falling in around them, Miller's protagonists seek, or are offered advice. They never take it. Some of their advisors serve as surrogate fathers. All become spokesmen for Miller, offering solutions that could prevent tragedies and revealing the characters' fatal flaws.

Willy periodically asks his neighbor Charley for advice. In their first scene, as they play cards, Willy confuses Charley with his brother Ben, whose advice he also seeks, stating, "For a second there you reminded me of my brother Ben." Willy's pride prevents him from accepting Charley's job offer although he borrows money from him each week, pretending to Linda it is his pay. Charley suggests that Willy go to his sons for help, but Willy cannot swallow his pride before those whom he wants most to impress. Charley points out, "The only thing you got in this world is what you can sell. And the funny thing is that you are a salesman, and you don't know that." He tells Willy to let Biff go, and when Willy hints at suicide in order to leave Biff his life insurance money, Charley is quick to say, "Nobody's worth nothin' dead." Charley is full of good advice, but Willy barely hears him, unwilling to relinquish any part of his dream and determined against every odd to make it come true.

In *Sons*, George advises his sister Ann to abandon the Keller household and return her loyalty to their father, falsely imprisoned and shunned due to Joe Keller's deceit. Ann stays, hoping to marry Chris. Their future is uncertain once she reveals Larry's letter and Joe shoots himself. In *Bridge*, Alfieri, a lawyer who acts as narrator, tells Eddie to let his niece go, that nothing in the law can prevent her from marrying an illegal immigrant. But Eddie cannot gain control over his desire, and Alfieri knows "where [Eddie is] heading for. Where he [is] going to end." Eddie's lust and pride prevent him from diverting his path. Giving up neither, he commits suicide on Marco's knife, leaving an uncertain future for Marco, Rodolpho, Catherine, and Beatrice. In *The Price*, Solomon replaces Victor and Walter's father, who has died sixteen years earlier. He urges them not to be so suspicious and to get along with each other. But the brothers cannot let go of the perspectives and feelings they have harbored for sixteen years, and they fail to reconcile. In *Morgan*, Lyman's lawyer, Tom, acts as a sounding board for Lyman and gives advice to Theo. He asks Lyman what he wants to do now that his bigamy has been discovered although he tells him that he has "done these women terrible harm." Later in the play, Tom informs Lyman that he can probably still choose one of his two wives to keep, but eventually, he challenges Lyman, stating that he purposely moved the barrier so that he would get caught. Tom offers his help to Theo, telling her to leave Lyman, and informs Lyman that he can no longer represent him. In *Broken Glass*, Dr. Hyman advises Gellburg to love his wife, an intimate suggestion which underscores Gellburg's impotency and guilt. Gellburg tries, but his attempts to change the course of his marriage are ineffectual. Further, he is threatened by the apparent mutual attraction between his wife and Dr. Hyman.[13]

All people carry emotional baggage. Their present interactions with others do not happen in a void. They are not talking with just those present but are all too aware of other voices in their heads. Miller has always known this, leading him to create protagonists who interact with the voices which haunt them. Some of these voices are embodied on stage, conjured, as it were by the protagonist; others never appear but are represented by another character or a stage property.

In *Salesman*, Willy conjures Uncle Ben, begging for information about his father, advice about how to raise his sons, and for assurance that he is doing the right thing. That all of these conversations occur in Willy's mind brings to question how much Ben actually has said and how much Willy attributes to him. The Woman also haunts Willy but for different reasons. Her laughter overrides Linda's compliments, which, in light of his adultery, Willy feels are undeserved. As he begins his descent, he recalls the night in Boston with The Woman which destroyed his dreams for his son Biff.

All characters in *After the Fall* are conjured by Quentin in his review of his life, which he is compelled to understand. In *Clara*, projections of her bloodied body flash in her father's mind as he deals with the shock of her murder. He recalls scenes with her which might give him clues as to what led to her death and the extent of his culpability. In *Morgan*, the appearances of Lyman's father indicate deep-seated conflicts between father and son, which still terrorize Lyman and prompt him to continually prove his manhood. Finally, in *Mr. Peters' Connections*, half of the characters are conjured by the protagonist; they have either died or, in the case of Adele, are "neither dead or alive," leaving Mr. Peters to question the nature of reality.

Significant absent characters are prevalent in Miller's plays. They are clearly represented on stage, and their impact on the characters' current conflicts is apparent. They serve as signifiers to the audience and characters, and often are reminders of the origins of the conflicts. Willy speaks to his former boss, Frank, who does not appear, in a scene in which "the light on his chair grows very bright and strange," and recalls his father, represented by flute music. In *Sons*, Steve Deever, wrongfully imprisoned, is represented on stage when George wears his hat in order to tell his sister they have misjudged him. Larry is represented by a tree planted too early in his memory. It blows over the night before the play begins, ominously foreshadowing his family learning that he has, indeed, died. In *The Price*, Victor and Walter's father is represented by Solomon, by the chair in the center of the stage, by the skylight overhead—as if he is watching from heaven—and by the laughing record a haunting, ironic laugh to Victor's ears. Their mother is represented by the harp her father gave her for a wedding present—it now has a cracked sounding board—and by her dresses which Walter considers giving to his own daughter. In *Ceiling*, that the room might be bugged impacts the characters' conversations; it is unclear whether or not "they" have heard anything in the room which causes them to first confiscate and then return Sigmund's manuscript. Angel is terrified in *Love Story* by cops who she claims are parked on the street watching her. In *Elegy*, the Proprietess replaces The Man's dying lover; by the end of the play the two have nearly merged into one. And, in *I Can't Remember Anything*, Leonora's husband has died, and she spends her evenings with his best friend, each replacing the loved one s/he has lost.

The complex web of thematic dichotomies and character conflicts in Miller's plays presents a challenge to embrace them within a theatrical structure. Miller has continually sought to create such a structure. He has utilized three major ones: multiple locales, single locales, and "plays of the mind." Those plays which use multiple locales also occur over a period of days, weeks, even months: *No Villain, They Too Arise, The Grass Still Grows, The Great Disobedience, The Golden Years, The Man Who Had All the Luck, An Enemy of the People, The Crucible, A View from the Bridge, Creation of the World and Other Business, The American Clock*, and *Broken Glass*. (*Half Bridge* is the exception, occurring within a twenty four hour period.) Those using a singular locale also occur in real time: *The Price, The Archbishop's Ceiling, Some Kind of Love Story, Elegy for a Lady, I Can't Remember Anything*, and *An Incident at Vichy*. There are a few exceptions: *Sons* actually occurs in approximately eighteen hours; *A Memory of Two Mondays* has two scenes in real time in two seasons; and *The Last Yankee* has two locales set in two scenes in real time, portions of which overlap. Finally, Miller has created plays of the mind, which use flexible, multiple locales, and time periods, as well as an element of subjective reality and fantasy: *Death of a Salesman, After the Fall, Clara, The Ride Down Mt. Morgan*, and *Mr. Peters' Connections*. In these plays, Miller has moved from presenting the past impinging upon the present, to presenting their simultaneity. In the opening stage directions for *After the Fall*, Miller refers to: "the flitting, instantaneousness of a mind" in a play which reveals the surrealistic processes of the subconscious and the struggle of the conscious mind to engage logic and reason. In its production, he was finally able to see realized the kind of set he had envisioned twenty four years earlier as he wrote *The Golden Years*, one which used platforms, lighting, and minimal properties.

What distinguishes Miller from other playwrights is his intent to bend time, to coin a phrase from his autobiography *Timebends*. He also bends place, a necessity if characters' minds are to freely move where they will, as they automatically and subconsciously make connections among different points of their lives. To all of this, Miller places one more demand upon his structure: the exploration of a man's mind and the ways in which memory is infiltrated by illusion and fantasy. This third demand, while accomplished on page by stream-of-conscious novelists, is much more difficult to realize on stage.

Salesman was a landmark in American drama, not only because of its universal themes and character which hit home with audiences, but also because in it, Miller created a structure which went beyond realism, embracing multiple time periods and locations, as well as revealing the interior conflicts in a man's mind. Beginning with *Death of a Salesman*, Miller has created dramatic structures which have challenged theatrical realism and strained towards a theatre of flexibility. Critics have argued about the dramaturgy of *Salesman*, some claiming it to be realism, others expressionism, and still others impressionism. That these "isms" are under scrutiny reveals Miller's focus on the central content of the play, rather than an embrace of a single formalistic method. While *Salesman* occurs within twenty-four hours, it includes multiple times and places as Willy's reality and memories collide and fuse, blend and confuse. In addition to the present, the play contains Willy's memories of his brother and father, his sons during high school, and his adultery. These occur in nine locales: four rooms in the Loman house, Charley's and Howard's offices, the Boston hotel room, Frank's Chop House, and the Lomans' back yard. Miller writes, "The structure of the play was determined by what was needed to draw up [Willy's] memories like a mass of tangled roots without end or beginning. This provides a sense of climax because if I could make him remember enough he would kill himself."

Salesman's universality is evident not only in its thematic content and characters, but also in the continuing challenges and opportunities it affords designers and directors realizing them on stage. From its landmark stage design in the 1949 Broadway premiere to its recent design for the fiftieth anniversary Broadway production, the play has been open to new visual and aural interpretations which reflect changes in the acceptance of design approaches by theatre practitioners and audiences alike. From its inception, *Salesman* has challenged theatre artists in its inherent requisites for staging. Miller had avoided the problems in multiple locales, the scene changes for which he believed were largely responsible for the failure of his first Broadway play, *The Man Who Had All the Luck*, in 1944 (Miller, *Timebends* 103) by utilizing a single setting in *All My Sons* three years later. He returned to multiple locales in *Salesman* augmented by multiple temporal changes occurring both within and outside of a man's consciousness. Miller's "play of the mind" began as numerous images, both visual and thematic: "a little frame house. . .[now]empty and silent and finally occupied by strangers. . ." (Martin and Centola 141-42). His first conception of his new play, which was to be entitled *The Inside of His Head*, arose "from structural images. The play's eye was to revolve with Willy's head, sweeping endlessly in all directions like a light on a sea, and nothing formed in the mist was to be left uninvestigated . . ." (Rowe 67-68). In a notebook he kept while writing the play, Miller jotted, "A fantasmagoria [sic]—many transitions."[14] Next he conceived "of an enormous face the height of the proscenium arch which would appear and then open up, and we would see the inside of Willy's skull. . .[who] would be crawling around, playing these scenes inside of himself."[15]

Although several producers and theatre practitioners rejected Miller's new work because they "did not see how the play could work theatrically" (Murphy 13), producer Kermit Bloomgarden, director Elia Kazan, and designer Jo Mielziner quickly accepted the theatrical challenge. As the collaboration began, Miller wrote a note to director Elia Kazan, describing the play's opening: "A pinpoint traveling spotlight hits a small area stage left. The Salesman is revealed. He takes out his keys and opens an invisible door" (Murphy 10). Miller envisaged an abstract production approach that was to be "without any setting at all . . . [using] three unadorned platforms and only the minimum necessary furniture"(Murphy 10).

A second version of the script Miller gave Mielziner reads, "The action takes place in Willy Loman's house—its bedrooms, kitchen, basement, front porch, and back yard, and in various offices and places of his visitation in New York City, today."[16] But his vision was poetic as well. In a note to Mielziner, he wrote: "[The house] had once been surrounded by open country, but it was now hemmed in with apartment houses. Trees that used to shield the house against the open sky and hot summer sun now were for the most part dead or dying"(Mielziner 25). Kazan later reported, "At the end of his forty-odd scenes Miller says, 'The scenic solution to this production will have to be an imaginative and simple one. I don't know the answer, but the designer must work out something which makes the script flow easily" (Mielziner 24). Miller concurs: "Mielziner took my three platforms and designed an environment around them, romantic, dream-like, lower middle-class, emblem of present versus past" (Miller *Timebends* 188).

A central question of Miller's drama, "How may a man make of the outside world a home?" (Martin and Centola 7) has led him to set all but four of his plays, for the most part, in homes, often in "disguised," if not actual, living rooms; designers have largely followed his lead. However, early in his career, Miller disparaged the value of the living room as a setting of a "natural" play, writing in a notebook, "Modern life has broken out of the living room."[17] In an essay about realism, he asked, "Would a real set make [a play] realistic? Not likely" (Martin and Centola 78). Although it is apparent from reading his plays that Miller's settings are precisely rooted in time and place, he wrote in an early notebook, "The object of scene design ought not be to reference a locale but to raise it into a significant statement."[18]

An early draft of *The Golden Years* written in 1940 reveals Miller's staging preference for platforms and lighting: A note on settings: a system of permanent or semi-permanent levels seems to provide the best method of setting the play. Very few properties are used. With the aid of imaginative lighting and such a system of levels, the scenes would be played one out of the other and the fluidity of the action would thereby be enhanced."[19] He has restaged his own works, *The Crucible*, for example, using only a cyc and tunnels of light (Roudane 25). Fifty-one years after *Golden Years*, in *The Ride Down Mt. Morgan*, Miller writes, "Notwithstanding the present stage directions, the play may be performed in open space with scenes separated by light and arrangements of furniture and props."

Jo Mielziner succeeded in not only designing a set which would allow for location and temporal changes, but one which created a significant metaphor for theme and character. Echoing an observation in Miller's notebook for *Salesman* that "a play designs its own set,"[20] Enoch Brater writes, "The set is the play" (Martin 119). Extending this parallel between set and play, Mielziner felt that "the most important visual symbol in the play—the real background of the story—was the Salesman's house" (Mielziner 25).

For *Salesman*, Mielziner designed a "skeletonized" structure of a house revealing three of its interior rooms: the kitchen, boys' bedroom, and parents' bedroom. Seats were removed at the expense of selling seats, in order to allow sufficient room on the forestage and apron for backyard scenes, and for furniture to be brought on quickly and easily for Howard's and Charley's offices, Frank's Chop House, the Boston hotel room, and, finally, the cemetery for the Requiem (Murphy 2). Spots and other lighting techniques were used to focus audience attention on the relevant parts of the stage. Temporal changes were designated by music, lighting, costume changes, and the ways in which actors used the set. As Miller writes at the beginning of the play, "Whenever the action is in the present the actors observe the imaginary wall-lines, entering the house only through its door at the left. But in scenes of the past these boundaries are broken, and characters enter or leave a room by stepping 'through' a wall onto the forestage." Mielziner and Eddie Kook utilized three projections, a relatively new theatrical technique: green leaves for scenes in the past, autumnal leaves for scenes in the present, and wallpaper for the Boston hotel room scene. Lighting changes effected a sense of continuous action, using a "cross fading" technique similar to that in film. There were reportedly 151 lighting cues in the production, which used more lighting sources than most musicals (Miller, *Timebends* 190). Mielziner and Eddie Kook "once worked an entire afternoon to light" Howard's chair (Miller *Timebends* 190).

The most unusual element of the *Salesman* production was the incorporation of music. Composed by Alex North, the music, performed by only four musicians (playing C and alto flutes, B flat and bass clarinets, trumpet, and cello)[21] was only 22 1/2 minutes in total, but there was a sense of the music being continuous. Critic Robert Bagar of the *New York World Telegraph* called the play "an unsung operatic tragedy" and "a symphonic work," the music operating as "an integral part of the whole."[22]

The major themes and characters which *Death of a Salesman* shares with other Miller plays were expressed by this original set, lighting, and music. Willy's mutually effective worlds of home and work are both presented on stage and in the contrast between his house and the surrounding new world: "the blue light of the sky [which] falls [only] upon the house and the forestage . . . the small, fragile-seeming home. An air of the dream clings to the place, a dream rising out of reality"—is juxtaposed with the outside world as manifested by the "towering angular shapes behind it, surrounding it on all sides," "the surrounding area shows an angry glow of orange," and "a solid vault of apartment houses."

The house alternately becomes a haven to which the exhausted, failed salesman returns, supported, even indulged by his wife Linda, and a place of reckoning as his son Biff challenges him to relinquish his fantasies and face the truth. Willy's guilt, which he denies and ultimately is forced to acknowledge, is revealed largely through properties: "the gas heater [which] begins to glow through the kitchen wall," the rubber tubing Linda tells Biff about, which he finds and confronts Willy with, and the stockings which Willy cannot tolerate Linda mending because they point to his inability to support her sufficiently and because they remind him of his adultery. As Biff cries, "You gave her Mama's stockings!"

The sense of reality versus dreams and illusions was signified by light and music changes as Willy slips into past scenes augmented through memory. The rural versus urban and the past versus the present were designated by the haunting music of his father's flute and by the trees which have long since been cut down to make way for the new apartment buildings. The symbolic trees are reminiscent of the tree planted for Larry in *Sons*.

Properties are aligned with specific characters and join musical motifs—of which there were eight in the premiere production—to identify and reveal character. The play, in fact, begins, "A flute is heard in the distance, soft, beguiling, memorable. [Willy] hears it but is not aware of it. It plays a tiny melody of grass and trees and the horizon." This is the salesmen's theme, recalling Willy's distant and vague memory of his father and ultimately becoming his own haunting theme. Music announced Willy's conjuring of Ben and The Woman. The Woman's music was played on bass clarinet and trumpet, while Linda's music was a hummed lullaby. The boys' music had multiple instrumentation, and Ben's was played on trumpet. Willy is signified by his "two large sample cases," which are too heavy for him to carry any longer. When Howard asks him to return the samples, he is, in effect, asking him to hand in his life. Biff is represented by numerous properties: the silver athletic trophy in Willy's bedroom, the "golden pool of light" and helmet, his football, the sneakers on which he has printed "University of Virginia," and the pen he steals from Bill Oliver.

The skeletal walls and extensive use of lighting and music were relatively new in mainstream Broadway theatre of 1949. *Salesman*'s creators relinquished architectural detail in favor of a setting which allowed audiences to peer into Willy's mind. The minimal selection of objects heightened their significance. In many ways, this presented a return to Greek and Elizabethan staging, now augmented with twentieth-century technology.

The Mielziner set was so effective a landmark that it has been emulated and adapted in virtually every *Salesman* production around the world. Productions in other countries often bear the imprint of a cultural stamp upon their designs. A production of *Salesman* which opened in Sweden on October 10, 1949, for example, exhibited a modernized, Scandinavian design nearly identical to the Broadway groundplan.[23] In the National Theatre of Taipei, Taiwan, in 1992, the set was virtually the same as the Broadway 1949 production. (Diamond 110). The design has followed the play for the past fifty years with rare departures.

Two departures stand out, though, which, in fact, more closely reflect Miller's original concept and images of the play and the acceptance of theatre practitioners to design possibilities.

In the 1996 National Theatre production in London, designer Fran Thompson created one such departure. The Mielziner design has become such a metaphor for the play that as the curtain opened, members of the National Theatre production audience were heard to whisper, "Where's the house? This is a play about a house."[24] The stage floor consisted of three concentric circles, two acting as revolves. The set represented *The Inside of His Head*, Miller's working title for the play, and created a space for the various worlds of Willy's life. Locations were set with minimal furnishings placed on the revolves, adding Charley's living room to the locations presented in the premiere production. Because the characters who haunt Willy are omnipresent, with few exceptions, actors remained on stage throughout the play. As Willy moved and remembered, the revolves turned so that the appropriate furnishings and characters moved into place downstage center. The center circle remained still and contained a large tree, the trunk of which had a large section cut out. This, and the red Chevy half buried in the stage floor, reflected Willy's demise. Ben sat in a chair upstage right, walking into the scenes as needed. The Woman, whose dialogue and laughter overlap Linda's and haunt Willy, was suspended in a bed upstage left. The bed lowered gradually and nearly imperceptibly until it reached the stage floor for the penultimate scene in the play when Biff catches his father in the Boston hotel room. A door upstage center allowed Ben to lure Willy to his death.

Rural and urban, old and new, were designated by lighting. Designer Rick Fisher used black and white for present-day scenes, casting large shadows of the tree and the characters on the side walls of the stage.[25] He flooded the stage with reds, blues, greens and yellows for Willy's' memories. Properties, which were similar to the premiere production, and costumes were stored around the set; for example, on the furniture, in suitcases under the beds, and in the car.

Composer Adrian Johnston held close to Alex North's music, out of respect for Miller's script.[26] He retained the motifs for the characters, extending the original instrumentation to include keyboards by taking advantage of modern technology.

The fiftieth anniversary Broadway production, intentionally or coincidentally, used concentric circles, as the National Theatre production had, but added two cubes which swung into various positions on stage. These served to accentuate the chaos of Willy's mind and his distorted, disintegrating vision of reality, as parts of his world floated in and out of his consciousness in a seemingly random pattern. One cube held Willy and Linda's bedroom, doubling ironically as the Boston hotel room; the other cube contained part of the Loman kitchen. As Willy's thoughts become increasingly fragmented, for example, the cube moved upstage right, while the kitchen table remained on the revolve downstage left. The set, designed by Mark Wendland, allowed characters to appear throughout the proscenium space, including on a high platform at the rear of the stage, on top of the cubes, and descending the stairs between them. The set was darkly lit, as critic Ben Brantley noted, "always threatening to consume Willy."[27] Designer Michael Philippi used blinding lights aimed at the audience to open the show as Willy arrives home in his car. Striking beams of light amidst the dark, and gobos denoting light coming through blinds and leaves, and a grid pattern on the stage floor, emphasized the harsh reality of Willy's world. Richard Woodbury's sound design included horns and drums to replace the flute music at the beginning of the play, creating a much harsher sense of Willy Loman's world. He also incorporated electronic sounds and music, dissonance, and amplified voices, adding to the chaotic nature of Willy's mind and the intrusion of guilt and panic.

The significant accomplishments which Miller, Kazan, Mielziner, and Kook achieved with *Salesman* have made the theatrical realization of other plays possible. One only need compare *The Man Who Had All the Luck* in 1944 on Broadway and its clumsy scene changes with *Broken Glass* fifty years later, in which a metaphoric environment was created by designer Santo Loquasto, with minimal furnishings and properties brought quickly on stage. Comparing Miller's early draft of *The Golden Years* in 1940 with *The Ride Down*

Mt. Morgan, in 1991 reveals that, in terms of staging, Miller has not changed his focus. Designers have continued their attempts to create sets which capture the essence of Miller's drama. The premiere of *After the Fall* used his preferred platforms and lighting, but did not allow for instantaneous entrances. He was happier with Zeffirelli's production, the design for which was "as though one were looking into the back of a bellows camera" (Martin and Centola 288), allowing for characters to appear and disappear anywhere at any time. Michael Blakemore's London production in 1991 consisted of an enormous spiral tilted at such an angle, so as to allow its surface to be acted upon.[28] Its shape reflected the "Golden Mean" found in nature and served as a metaphoric environment in which Quentin attempts to understand his life in order to move forward.

Although Boris Aronson had wanted to use his constructivist view to create the setting for *The Price* in 1968 by cutting up and rebuilding pieces of furniture, realism prevailed.[29] In the 1997 Guthrie Theatre Production, Fran Thompson used reverse perspective to create a mound of furniture growing ever larger and tilting threateningly over the characters. Abstract plays such as *Elegy for a Lady* encourage abstract, symbolic sets. The fluidity of *The American Clock* demands that properties be rolled on and off stage upon characters' entrances and exits, although the Signature Theatre Company's 1998 production abandoned the significant piano and bicycle, characters miming both. Audience imagination filled the void.[30]

Miller has used music in all but one of his published plays. His scripts and their productions reflect his preference for jazz, albeit, at times, anachronistic. Songs of the period are endemic to *American Clock*, the cello hauntingly bridges scenes in *Broken Glass*, and, increasingly, composers like Barrington Pheloung for *Morgan* underscore scenes, much as they would do in films.[31]

Upon his success with *Salesman*, Miller did not develop a formula but, instead, continued to develop methods by which to explore and express a man's mind and soul. Each play, for all its similarities, differs; thus, it is impossible to label Miller or designate periods, although critics have tried. There are patterns in Miller's drama in terms of theme, character, structure and form, and staging, developed by directorial and designer collaboration. But it is the subtleties within those patterns which reveal Miller's persistent, continued, intense, and personal exploration of fundamental elements of the human condition and archetypal characters which echo in the Greek drama he revered so early in his playwrighting career.

Miller has created a home for himself around the world through his plays, the universality of which, as with *Salesman*, continues, even as they continue to challenge directors, designers, actors, and audiences, providing opportunities to create and to understand. In a world changing at an increasingly fast pace—instant news and information through the media and internet, divorce rates and changing family structures, borders moving between countries—the need has become even greater to understand the interplay between internal thoughts, desires, and dreams, and external actions of others, as well as man/woman's struggle against alienation, so that attention is, indeed, paid. Evidence shows that we still have not found solutions, and so, there are Willy Lomans around the world living the tragedy of the human condition.

A view from *Death of a Salesman* reveals that it is a great play among many, by a man who insists upon addressing fundamental issues of human existence and continually searches for a theatrical form which expresses the human mind and soul as it attempts to "make of the world a home."

Notes

[1] Phrase coined by Thorstein Veblen, *Theory of the Leisure Class*, (New York: Penguin Books, 1979).
[2] Unpublished manuscripts and papers on deposit at the Harry Ransom Humanities Research Center, The University of Texas at Austin.
[3] See also *The Crucible*.
[4] See also *The American Clock* and *The Ride Down Mt. Morgan*.
[5] See also *Honors at Dawn, All My Sons, An Enemy of the People, The Crucible, A View from the Bridge, After the Fall, The American Clock, The Archbishop's Ceiling, Some Kind of Love Story, Clara, I Can't Remember Anything, The Ride Down Mt. Morgan*, and *The Last Yankee*.
[6] See also *They Too Arise, The Golden Years, All My Sons, A View from the Bridge, After the Fall, The American Clock, Elegy for a Lady, Some Kind of Love Story, I Can't Remember Anything, Clara, The Ride Down Mt. Morgan, The Last Yankee*, and *Mr. Peters' Connections*.
[7] See also *The Price, The Creation of the World and Other Business, Elegy for a Lady, Clara*, and *Broken Glass*.
[8] Miller states that he still does not know whether David should have committed suicide in *The Man Who Had All the Luck*.

[9] See also *Honors at Dawn, The Man Who Had All the Luck,* and *A View from the Bridge.*
[10] On deposit at the Harry Ransom Humanities Research Center, The University of Texas at Austin
[11] See also *After the Fall, The Archbishop's Ceiling, Elegy for a Lady, The Last Yankee,* and *Mr. Peters' Connections.*
[12] See also *An Enemy of the People* and *A Memory of Two Mondays.*
[13] See also *The Golden Years, An Enemy of the People, The Crucible, Incident at Vichy, After the Fall, The Archbishop's Ceiling,* and *Elegy for a Lady.*
[14] On deposit at the Harry Ransom Humanities Research Center, The University of Texas at Austin.
[15] On deposit at the Harry Ransom Humanities Research Center, The University of Texas at Austin
[16] On deposit at the Harry Ransom Humanities Research Center, The University of Texas at Austin.
[17] On deposit at the Harry Ransom Humanities Research Center, The University of Texas at Austin.
[18] On deposit at the Harry Ransom Humanities Research Center, The University of Texas at Austin.
[19] On deposit at the Harry Ransom Humanities Research Center, The University of Texas at Austin.
[20] On deposit at the Harry Ransom Humanities Research Center, The University of Texas at Austin.
[21] On deposit at the Harry Ransom Humanities Research Center, The University of Texas at Austin.
[22] Robert Bagar, *New York World Telegraph,* March 26, 1949; Clipping on deposit at the Harry Ransom Humanities Research Center, The University of
[23] On deposit at the Harry Ransom Humanities Research Center, The University of Texas at Austin.
[24] Fran Thompson, personal interview, 2 June 1998; Archival materials on deposit at the National Theatre Archives, London.
[25] Rick Fisher, personal interview, 1 July 1999.
[26] Adrian Johnston, personal interview, 14 May 1999.
[27] Ben Brantley, *New York Times,* February 11, 1999.
[28] Michael Blakemore, personal interview, 2 July 1999.
[29] Lisa Aronson, personal interview, 14 April 1999.
[30] James Houghton, personal interview, 9 April 1999.
[31] Barrington Pheloung, personal interview, 16 June 1999.

Works Cited

Aronson, Lisa. Personal interview. 14 April 1999.
Bagar, Robert. *New York World Telegraph,* March 26, 1949.

Brantley, Ben. *New York Times*, February 11, 1999.

Blakemore, Michael. Personal interview. 2 July 1999.

Diamond, Catherine. *Death of a Salesman. Theatre Review.*

Fisher, Rick. Personal interview. 1 July 1999.

Harry Ransom Humanities Research Center, University of Texas at Austin.

Houghton, James. Personal interview. 9 April 1999.

Johnston, Adrian. Personal interview. 14 May 1999.

Martin, Robert A. *Arthur Miller: New Perspectives.* Englewood Cliffs, NJ: Prentice-Hall, Inc., 1982.

Martin, Robert A. and Steven R. Centola, eds. *The Theater Essays of Arthur Miller.* New York: Da Capo Press, 1996.

Mielziner, Jo. *Designing for the Theater: A Memoir and Portfolio.* New York: Athenaeum, 1965.

Miller, Arthur. *Timebends.* New York: Grove Press, 1987.

Miller, Arthur. *Salesman in Beijing.* London: Methuen, 1983.

Murphy, Brenda. *Miller: Death of Salesman (Plays in Production).* Cambridge: Cambridge University Press, 1995.

Parker, Brian. "Point of View in Arthur Miller's *Death of a Salesman.*" *Arthur Miller's Death of a Salesman.* Harold Bloom, ed. New York: Chelsea House Publishers, 1988.

Pheloung, Barrington. Personal interview. 16 June 1999.

Roudane, Matthew C., ed. *Conversations with Arthur Miller.* London: University Press of Mississippi, 1987.

Rowe, Kenneth Thorpe. *A Theater in Your Head.* New York: Funk & Wagnalls. 1960.

Taubman, Howard. *The New York Times*, March 27, 1949.

Thompson, Fran. Personal interview. 2 June 1998.

Veblen, Thorstein. *Theory of the Leisure Class.* New York: Penguin Books, 1979.

Notes to Preface

Brantley, Ben. "Attention Must Be Paid, Again." *New York Times* 11 Feb. 1999, E 1.

Clive, Barnes. "*Salesman* is Still a Seller." *New York Post* 14 Feb. 1999.

Miller, Arthur. "The *Salesman* Has a Birthday." *New York Times* 5 Feb. 1950.

---. Letter to Stephen Marino. 13 April 1999.

---. "Preface: *Salesman* at Fifty." In *Death of a Salesman* 50th Anniversary Edition. New York: Penguin, 1999.

---. *Timebends, A Life*. New York: Grove Press, 1987.

O'Toole, Fintan. "*Death of a Salesman*" is Sensational." *New York Daily News* 11 Feb. 1999.

Pacheco, Patrick. "Arthur Miller and the Life of a Playwright." *Newsday* 12 Nov. 1999

Winer, Linda. "Everyman Revisited." *Newsday* 12 Feb. 1999.

Index

Note: Some entries that appear throughout the book, such as *Death of a Salesman*, Willy Loman, and Arthur Miller are not fully listed in the index.

Contributors

SUSAN C. W. ABBOTSON teaches at Rhode Island College. She has published essays on drama in the *South Atlantic Review*, *English Studies*, *American Drama*, and *Modern Drama*. She is the co-author, with Brenda Murphy, of *Understanding Death of a Salesman*, from the Literature in Context series of Greenwood Press. Her new book is *The Student Companion to Arthur Miller*, also from Greenwood Press. She is vice president of The Arthur Miller Society.

CHRISTOPHER BIGSBY is Professor of American Studies at the University of East Anglia. He has published more than twenty books on British and American culture including *Confrontation and Commitment: A Study of Contemporary American Drama*; *A Critical Introduction to Twentieth Century American Drama* (three volumes); and *Modern American Drama 1940-1990*. His books on Arthur Miller include *Arthur Miller and Company*, *The Portable Arthur Miller*, and *The Cambridge Companion to Arthur Miller*. He is also the author of three novels: *Hester*, *Pearl*, and *Still Lives*.

HEATHER COOK CALLOW received her Ph.D. from Johns Hopkins University. She has been a visiting professor in Japan and Taiwan and Fulbright Lecturer to Saudi Arabia. Currently she is assistant professorial lecturer at the George Washington University in Washington, D.C. A Joyce scholar, her articles have appeared in *The James Joyce Quarterly*, *Twentieth-Century Literature*, and *The Journal of Narrative Technique*.

GEORGE P. CASTELLITTO is Professor of English and Director of the Graduate Program in English at Felician College in New Jersey. He received his Ph.D. from Fordham University. He has published articles on the use of images in the works of Wallace Stevens, William Carlos Williams, and Martin Scorsese. He is the editor of *The Journal of Imagism*.

STEVEN R. CENTOLA is Professor of English at Millersville University in Millersville, Pennsylvania. He is the founder of The Arthur Miller Society and served as its first president. He is the author of several articles on Miller, three interviews with the playwright and three books: *Arthur Miller in Conversation*, *The*

Achievement of Arthur Miller, and the revised and expanded version of the *Theatre Essays of Arthur Miller*. He has also completed *The Critical Response to Arthur Miller* and is working on a collection of the non-theater essays of Arthur Miller.

JANE K. DOMINIK teaches at San Joaquin Delta College in Stockton, California. She holds an M.A. from The University of Chicago, an M.F.A. from Rutgers University, and is completing a dissertation on Arthur Miller at the University of East Anglia. She is the editor of The Arthur Miller Society Newsletter and has presented numerous conference papers on Miller and other playwrights.

PETER LEVINE is a Professor of American Studies at Michigan State University where he directs the American Studies program. He is the author of many books including *Ellis Island to Ebbets Field: Sport and the American Jewish Experience*; *American Sport, A Documentary History*, and *Idols of the Game: A Sporting History of the American Century*, with Robert Lipsyte. His latest book is *The Rabbi of Swat*, his first novel.

STEPHEN A. MARINO teaches at Saint Francis College in Brooklyn, New York. His work on Arthur Miller has appeared in *The Journal of Imagism, Modern Drama*, and *The Crucible: Modern Critical Interpretations* (Chelsea House). His poetry has recently appeared in *America* and *The Saint Francis College Review*. He is the secretary/treasurer of The Arthur Miller Society.

BRENDA MURPHY is Professor of English at the University of Connecticut. She is the author of many books including: *Congressional Theatre: Dramatizing McCarthyism on Stage,. Film and Television*; *Miller: Death of a Salesman*; *Tennessee Williams and Elia Kazan: A Collaboration in the Theatre*; *American Realism and American Drama, 1880-1940*. She is editor of *Understanding Death of a Salesman*, with Susan Abbotson; *The Cambridge Companion to American Women Playwrights*; and *A Realism in the American Theatre: Selected Drama Criticism of William Dean Howells*. She is currently working on a book about Eugene O'Neill.

MATTHEW ROUDANÉ is Professor of English at Georgia State University in Atlanta. He has published many books on modern American drama including: *Conversations with Arthur Miller*,

Approaches to Teaching Miller's Death of a Salesman, and *American Drama since 1960: A Critical History.* He edited *The Cambridge Companion to Tennessee Williams* and is the editor of the *South Atlantic Review.*

stud finder

circuitals